Dyamond

in the

ROUGH

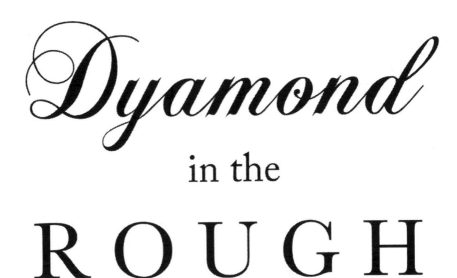

DYAMOND IN THE ROUGH

A COLLECTION OF REFLECTIONS
BY

DYME TAYLOR

Written *fluently* in Ebonics

This book belongs to:

_____

DYAMOND IN THE ROUGH

Dedication

This is for all my girls
who were never instilled with self-love because the roots of
their parents lacked the same love.
For all my girls with "ugly attitudes", who were betrayed and
scorned by the unthinkable
who are incarcerated mentally or physically because they took
their parents' problems upon themselves.
For all my girls who stay in and out of clinics because they
were never taught nor shown their value.
And the ones who are told "to get over it", but never given the
chance to set their truths free.

This is for all my girls,
interrupted.

Shout out to Aziah and all the "Zolas" in the world.
&
Shout out to Tasneem and all the Hoodrat Feminists.

REST IN PEACE
2
Taylor Crenshaw
aka
Nicole Milfie

Contents

Foreword

Dearest Dyamond,

According to the Merriam-Webster Dictionary the definition of diamond is a Mineral composed of pure CARBON, the hardest naturally occurring substance known and a valuable gemstone. Diamonds are formed deep in the Earth by tremendous pressures and temperatures over long periods of time. Diamonds vary from colorless to black and may be transparent, translucent, or opaque. Most gem diamonds are transparent and colorless or nearly so. Because of their extreme hardness, diamonds have important industrial applications. In the symbolism of gemstones, the diamond represents steadfast love. How ironic!

I know, right about now you are thinking that I'm off on another tangent or you will recall our conversation about the significance of a name and how I firmly believe there is great meaning and correlation behind a person's name and character traits. You truly are a diamond and I pray that you only surround yourself with those whose light will allow you to shine and sparkle in every light. There are many students who walk through a teacher's classroom, but there are few students who make a profound impression upon a teacher. For those who have never had the privilege of meeting you then I can honestly say that they are missing out on meeting one of the most genuine women they will ever meet. If people only judge a book by its cover then they would never understand the complex story line in your book that looks like another "teen" story and they would miss out on a wonderful story; a story filled with heartaches, headaches, bumps, bruises, peaks and valleys, tears and laughter, lessons learned and lessons to be learned...the wonderful story of Dyamond.

Although I have only known you for a few short months, the time that I have interacted with you, have left the impression that you are wise beyond your years. You are not, by any stretch, a perfect student or teen, but the wonderful part about you is that when you realize you have made a mistake, you take ownership. In a time when most teens place blame on others rather than accepting the consequences for their choices YOU are the type of person who will *look to it as an opportunity to improve herself. When you asked me to write you a note in your Memory Book, I don't think you were expecting to receive a full page or more, single spaced, typed letter from me. I'm glad that the bell rang when it did so I could have the opportunity to write a heartfelt letter to you.*

I can't help but think back to our first week of school and I didn't know anything about you, and you knew nothing about me...at least that's what I would like to think. We had a brief, yet intense, exchange about how things were going to work in my classroom and after our exchange the whole class was staring at the two of us. I remember wondering what the heck; why are they all staring at us? Little did I know that our personalities are mirror images...you the younger version and I, of course, the older version.

You value those who not only talk the talk but walk the walk and because of that, most of your classmates' fear and respect you because of your honesty and zero tolerance for nonsense. As you know a majority of your high school classmate are immature, careless, self-centered, and can't see past today, but you are the one who puts things into perspective for them...I love it when other students say what I can't. You have never made excuses for why you couldn't get things done; you made excuses to get things done. There is no doubt in my mind that you will succeed in life. I would love for the opportunity to hear about all of the great things you have done with your life...of course in about 10 to 20 years.

Dyamond, you are the epitome of the saying "if there is a will, there is a way." Best wishes in all of your endeavors. And remember.... Make good choices. Be safe. Drink lots of water.

2013
  Mrs. Gavia

Preface

When my great aunt recently asked me what I wanted to do in life, I told her that I wanted to work with young girls at juvenile detention centers and homeless shelters. When I was finished talking, she paused and asked "What do you contribute to them?" Genuinely baffled, I asked her what she meant. She then snickered and said, "Exactly what I asked."

Now let's be real, I knew what the fuck she was asking. I just couldn't believe that my 88-year-old great aunt was really trying to read me — for filth. Immediately, I became defensive and thought "Are you stupid? Are you dumb?" However, I answered, "I know the feeling of being neglected and not wanted by your own parents" Challenging me again, she declared "—But you had your grandmother…"

In which I responded, "Although I'm grateful for my grandmother, her presence did not take away the everyday pain I had to endure when looking around at my peers with their mothers and fathers." She then argued "Well Dyamond, my mother died", as if I was supposed to sympathize with her, when she wasn't trying to empathize with me.

I said to her "Imagine having a well alive mother and father who are breathing in the same city as you and still don't give a fuck about you... which one do you think is worse?" I felt bad because at the end of the day she's still my great aunt…so I added "it doesn't really matter because both were out of our control."

Even after I remained open and told her I had been sad since I was 7 years old, further protesting she said, "I never saw you sad" as if I was lying. I asked "Why would you ever see me sad, when I came to your house during family holidays? Your house was somewhere I could see and play with all my cousins. It was an escape."

She asked me why I was still sad, and I told her because I have a personal flaw of dwelling in the past. Immediately, she became frustrated with me, "Well, why do you dwell in the past?? Because you want to pity yourself???"

NO— you old white bitch. I'M FUCKING TRAUMATIZED.

Fighting back tears of rage, I asked her "So, when you and my grandma speak about what your father use to do, it's called reminiscing... but who do I have to share my memories with? No one, so it's called dwelling." Memories that never fade, nightmares that always haunt me.

I was tired of her trying me, so I no longer held back. I continued to speak my mind "And see, I can't imagine... if I wasn't me. If I didn't have the strength, I have... how stupid you would have made me felt for feeling what I feel when I have every right to be sad because of everything I had to endure as a child. Do you know how many kids kill themselves because people, including their own families make them feel stupid or less than for feeling emotions, they did not cause themselves to feel in the first place?"

She could only respond by saying "Aww baby, I wasn't trying to make you feel that way... but at least you're ambitious. I can say that."

UM HELLO...
YOU CAN NOT TELL ANYBODY HOW THEY'RE
SUPPOSED TO FEEL OR ACT BECAUSE YOU REACTED
DIFFERENTLY IN YOUR OWN STRUGGLE.
KUDOS TO YOU FOR HAVING ENOUGH STRENGTH TO
MOVE PAST YOUR PAIN BUT NOT EVERYBODY IS LIKE YOU.
SOME OF US REFUSE TO MINIMIZE, BURY, OR DISMISS
OUR TRAUMA FOR OTHER'S COMFORT.

So, here's my Contribution:
When my great aunt asked me what I contributed to the type of young women I mentioned, I'll admit I didn't have a straight answer. I got frustrated and overwhelmed by my emotions. But after deep reflection and *dwelling* on our conversation, I now KNOW what I must contribute; something many girls are afraid to use,
A VOICE.

CHAPTER 1

How Much Pressure Does It Take to
Make a Dyamond?

MDD

I have a mental illness
that likes to use me as a puppet.
Times I feel no control over my emotions
is when it comes full throttle to take over my mind.
Why are you my best friend Depression?

Because when nobody else is...
You are.

Today I woke up
and felt nothing but disappointment,

Yet last night I felt untouchable!
What happened in my sleep?
Did I dream of happiness?

It comes when it wants
and leaves when it don't.

We first met when I was 9,
using that wire hanger to drag a horizontal line on my arm
that my parents never noticed,

And as I got older
it grew too.

Year after year,
Nothing I could do was a threat to this bitch!

Major Depressive Disorder
Unknown prescribed medication for my illness...
I'm not taking that shit!
Well to others yet frivolous to myself
Why the fuck am I living so reckless?
Suicidal and promiscuous
I make videos caressing my body parts
to feel closer to my heart.

Just so tomorrow can come around
and I hate every part of my life.
Don't want to get out of bed.
Don't even feel alive.
Don't have much to say today
because I'll just tell you lies.
"I'm just tired" or "I promise I'm fine"

Depression
Why are you my best friend?

I write to help ease the pain
I write to keep me lifted
because I can't get high enough to keep that mental illness
from catching me slipping

Damn this bitch is gifted.

DYAMOND IN THE ROUGH MEDICAL OFFICE

Taylor, Dyamond L
MRN:
DOB: 11/3/1994, Sex: F

DEPARTMENT OF PSYCHIATRY
OUTPATIENT INITIAL ADULT DIAGNOSTIC EVALUATION AND TREATMENT PLAN

PRESENTING PROBLEM: Dyamond L Taylor is seeking services today due to: symptoms of depression and anxiety

Patient states that she was referred to therapy to address sx of long-standing, chronic struggles with depression and anxiety, hx of sexual abuse and hx of self-injurious behaviors. She states, "My own demons are eating me inside. I've always been depressed. Maybe since like seven [years old]".

She adds that she used to engage in self-injurious behaviors to cope with feelings of overwhelm. She states that has "dragged a hanger" across her arm, used to "scratch the skin off" of her face and would cut her arm (sometimes the the point of losing consciousness). Pt admits to engaging in impulsive behaviors (i.e. unprotected sex with multiple partners).

SYMPTOMS EVALUATION
TREATMENT PROGRESS INDICATOR (TPI) - IF AVAILABLE
Behavioral Impairment Score (BHI):
59 PHQ 9 Score: 12
GAD 7 Score: 17

DEPRESSION: Depressed mood, sadness, irritable mood, decreased interest or pleasure, excessive guilt, feeling worthless, decreased energy / fatigue and feeling hopeless
ANXIETY/PANIC: Excessive worry or anxiety, difficulty controlling the worry, feeling keyed up or on edge, difficulty concentrating and sleep disturbance
MANIA: Excessive pleasurable activities with a high degree of risk
PTSD: Experienced, witnessed or was confronted with an event that involved death, serious injury, sexual violation or violent accident

WHAT HELPS DECREASE OR LESSEN SEVERITY OF PATIENT'S SYMPTOMS?: "Being around people that I like"

RISK ASSESSMENT/SAFETY

History of Self Injury: Yes, previous hx of cutting arm, excoriation.
History of Suicide Attempts: Yes, pt reports cutting herself until she "blacked out"
If suicidal risk is indicated, assess for protective factors or reasons for Living: Internal Factors: Ability to seek help
External Factors: Devotion to 7 month old daughter
What kept the patient from acting on previous suicidal thoughts: "Just didn't happen in the past. But now, I have my daughter"

4

DYAMOND IN THE ROUGH

Domestic Violence: Did you come here today because you were hurt by your current/past husband, boyfriend, girlfriend, partner? Yes
1. Within the last year, have you been pushed, shoved, hit, slapped, kicked, or otherwise physically hurt? No
2. Within the past year have you been forced to have sexual activities? No
3. Have you ever been emotionally or physically abused? Yes: Her senior year of high school, her boyfriend at the time would both physically and sexually abuse her
If indicated, assess for Military Trauma and/or History of Abuse: Physical and Sexual
Was this reported: Physical- Yes Sexual- NO

PSYCHIATRIC HISTORY (if indicated)
Previous Psychiatric Issues: MDD, PTSD
Outpatient Treatment: Yes, patient reports seeing a psychiatrist and a therapist in the 10th grade to cope with depression, insomnia and nightmares

SUBSTANCE USE ASSESSMENT
Current tobacco use: Denies
Current Use of other substances: Alcohol: amount 3 drinks per sitting, frequency 1-2x weekly and last used last week
Past Use of other substances: Patient denies but later comes clean about her opioid use

DYAMOND IN THE ROUGH

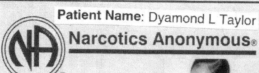

Patient Name: Dyamond L Taylor

Narcotics Anonymous®

Brief Substance Abuse Assessment

Substance Used:

Oxycodone

First use age 15:

Stole from an aunt with Cancer

Tramadol:

"My mother gives me her prescription"

Patient reports that her mother currently gives her tramadol

Currently uses twice a week.

Ecstasy,   IP No. 7   Norco,

Am I an   Morphene

Tramadol

Addict?

Maternal grandmother died
of heroine overdose in 1992

Mother told her at 15y.o.

"i had you to replace my mother"

3/30/2017

Hi, my name is Dyamond
and I'm an alcoholic addict.

I've been battling with addiction since I was 15 years old, but never seemed to notice.
I started taking hydrocodone and oxycodone in the 10th grade.
My aunt got them prescribed but didn't use them..
So, I would steal them.
I couldn't help but to notice in 12th grade that I started losing my memory.
Memories from a year or two ago would vanish. Slowly I began to lose memories day to day.

I was 18 years old when I graduated and moved back to LA.
My mother's boyfriend was a drug dealer, so I started to get them from him.
Occasionally, I would get them from my other aunt or my friends who had them.
I'd have them sometimes and sometimes I wouldn't.
Mostly Tramadol, Oxycodone, and Morphine.
If I had enough, I would take them every day.
I used them when I'd have to go out and needed to be social or when I was in school to make time go by much faster.

As far as my battle with drinking:
I choose not to drink often but when I do, I binge drink to the point of blacking out.
I become a whole other person.
My mood changes very quickly from happy and playful to extremely violent and full of rage.
I seem to hurt those I love, just like those who've hurt me.

Before the substances, cutting was my drug of choice.

I was 20 years old when I stopped cutting myself.

DYAMOND IN THE ROUGH

I got pregnant and vowed to never hurt myself ever again,
but after I gave birth it seemed like every day was a never-
ending battle with myself.

Trying to ignore the fact that my parents and my resentment
towards them was a trigger.
From steadily putting myself into situations with them that
would only result in me getting hurt to
passing certain streets in LA that would only cause me to
dwell.

I grew so tired of living in the pain I had been through
that I almost lost myself in the painful cycle.
I knew my fight to break this cycle of suffering wouldn't be
easy,
so, I started going back to therapy.
And therapy did help.
It helped me organize my everyday thoughts and stabilize my
moods.

What didn't help was that I wasn't truthful about a lot of things
in the beginning because
I was afraid they would try to take my daughter away,
but once I found the courage to confess
I did – well kind of.

My drug intake was indeed a problem,
but to me the bigger problem was that I never even got to the
root of why I was doing the drugs.

Sure, all my therapists and psychiatrists knew of what
happened to me when I was a child.
I told them the first day of evaluation,
but we never got into the depths of the things that happened.

It started to seem like every session was above the surface
and maybe it was partly my fault…

DYAMOND IN THE ROUGH

When I thought I was ready to talk about the depths of the
problems,
my therapist never asked.
Which only made me feel uncomfortable bringing any of it up,
because in all honesty, was I really ready to accept and own all
my painful truths?

DYAMOND IN THE ROUGH MEDICAL OFFICE

Taylor, Dyamond L
MRN:
DOB: 11/3/1994, Sex: F

Individual Follow-up Progress Note

Date: 1/12/2017

Procedure Code/Time spent: 90834: 45-50 minutes
Procedure description: Individual Psychotherapy

Dyamond L Taylor, 22 year old, female
had concerns including DEPRESSION.

SYMPTOMS: Major Themes/Subjective report: Patient reports that she has felt depressed and anxious her whole life. When parents saw that she started to cut herself in the 10th grade, she was referred to psych treatment in Texas, which was where she grew up. Pt wants mental health records from high school, "to start writing a book". Patient states " I'm in a weird space right now". Appears more depressed and more anxious than last visit. Couldn't articulate specifics that would cause it. "I know people need to hear my story, but I can't focus to write it and when I am I feel overwhelmed and crazy".

CHAPTER 2

Dyamond, A Woman's Best friend

DYAMOND IN THE ROUGH GUIDANCE CENTER   Circa 2011

Child and Adolesecent Mental Staus Examination
Dyamond Taylor
DOB: 11/3/94
Sex: F

Start Time: 6:00PM

I.   Appearance

Maturity:	__X__ appropriate	_____ immature	_____overly/pseudo mature
Dress:	_____appropriate	_____unkempt	__X__provocative ___meticulous
Speech:	__X__ articulate	_____poorly articulated	

II.   Mood and Affect

Depression:	_____none	_____ mild	_____moderate	__X__ severe
Elation:	__X__ none	_____ mild	_____moderate	_____ severe
Irritability:	_____none	_____ mild	_____moderate	__X__ severe

VI.   Suicidal Ideation

_____none
__X__wishes he/she were dead   __X__ suicidal plan, no intent to carry out
_____suicidal thoughts, no pain   _____clear intent to harm/kill self

Brief Summary of HPI:
17 y/o AAF brought to DITR by her uncle for depression. Pt reports, "I'm never happy".
Pt's uncle reports that pt was "abandoned" by her bio mother;
bio father is homeless and on drugs. Pt's parents willingly relinquished custody of her.

Diagnoses:
Generalized Anxiety D/O
r/o PTSD (second degree to child sexual abuse victim)
17 y/o AAF with consistent sxs of MDD, GAD, and suspected PTSD.
Second degree to childhood sexual abuse, exacerbated by multiple psychosocial factors.
second degree to parental neglect + subsequent relinquishment of her
custody to her paternal aunt.

Pt said she does not have a plan or want to kill herself;
she cuts so she can get the pain "out of my heart and so I won't hurt others."
Pt's mood was stable and she laughed and smiled several times in session.

Pt described herself as a "parentless child."
Stop Time: 6:50pm

CALIFORNIA COPY CERTIFICATION OF POWER OF ATTORNEY

State of California

County of _LOS ANGELES_ } ss.

On this the _16_ day of _Jan_, _2008_ I certify that the attached document is a true, complete and unaltered photocopy of a power of attorney presented

to me on this date by

X _Tina Floyd_
Name of Person Presenting Document

under Section 4307 of the California Probate Code.

NOTARY PUBLIC ∙ CALIFORNIA
LOS ANGELES COUNTY
Comm. Exp. NOV. 1, 2011

_____
Signature of Notary Public

Place Notary Seal Above

———— OPTIONAL ————

Though the information below is not required by law, it may prove valuable to persons relying on the power of attorney and could prevent fraudulent removal and reattachment of this form to another document.

Further Description of Attached Document

Title of Document: _Consent / Guardianship_

Name of Individual Granting Power of Attorney: _Tina Floyd_

Name of Individual Designated Attorney in Fact: _Dyamond Taylor_

Name of Entity Represented by Attorney in Fact, if Any: _____

Document Date: _1 16 08_ Number of Pages: _1_ County Where Recorded: _Los Angeles_

Where Original Document Kept: _____

Capacity Claimed by Custodian

☑ Individual
☐ Corporate Officer — Title: _____
☐ University or School Officer — Title: _____
☐ Governmental Officer or Agent — Title: _____
☐ Business Proprietor or Manager for_____
☐ Attorney for _____
☐ Trustee for _____
☑ Other: _Mother, Tina Floyd. Child. Dyamond Taylor_

RIGHT THUMBPRINT
OF PRESENTER
Top of thumb here

DYAMOND IN THE ROUGH GUIDANCE CENTER

Dyamond Taylor
DOB: 11/3/94
Sex: F

PROGRESS NOTE

Date: 11/20/2011

Start Time: 2:00pm

Pt was very irritable today.

She said she does not believe in Thanksgiving or Christmas, does not know what it is like to have "real family."

Pt thoughts and comments were very negative.

Pt said she got into a fight last week and cut herself last week.

Stop Time: 2:50pm

Thanksgiving

Where are the people I'm supposed to be thanking?

Mother?
Father?
Are you here?

NO.

I would've been thankful had my mother just abort.
Instead I'm growing up without my parents' love,
without their support

*Dyme Taylor LIVE on ABANDON YOUR KIDS NEWS
REPORT:*

"Here with a 16-year-old girl who's been sold short.
But she never makes excuses, so she says Fuck Yours"

If my parents were items
They'd be sold in discount stores.
I wish they had some value–

something I could be thankful for.

Celibacy

Born pure rushed into celibacy.
I never knew by 12 I would lust for a nigga
who had brown skin and was 6'3.
A nigga who was 4 years older than me
who got his PhD in T.H.C. with a minor felony.
Born pure rushed into celibacy.
My nigga loved to whisper in my ear how he only trusted me
and he was there so often that we made love until he fucked
me.
Born pure rushed into celibacy.
I never told him to stop once he started touching me
because I felt an urge of security every time, he'd thrust in me.
Born pure rushed into celibacy.
Everybody blamed my momma for corrupting me
but they never knew about the old nigga in the middle of the
night
disrupting me.
Born pure rushed into celibacy.
Who would've ever known an orgasm would be a drug to me
—an antidepressant mixed with a lot of morphine.
I was born pure rushed into celibacy, little did I know I knew
nothing.

2014

From: dyamondtaylor@yahoo.com
To: nikkihall5@yahoo.com
Date: 06/01/11 6:01pm
Subject: READ ALONE IN YOUR ROOM

Body:
Confessions of a Lonely Girl:

I wrote a poem called *Young* Hoe
It's a piece to my puzzle.
Here it goes:

Don't think I'm sick, I'm just a young girl who got taken up
quick
I'm not like my mother who looks for a profit
Instead
I got turned into an object
"Objection!!
Your Honor, This Girl is Only 12"
"Go On"
Ever since I was a little girl, all I ever knew about was sex
I guess my parents sexing in front of my innocent eyes was
never a threat
And I guess neither was me masturbating at 6 years old
imagining sex
All from what my memory kept
Ignorant to what I was doing to my body until I turned 12 and
started to get wet
Not realizing what I was about to do would later be something
down the line I regret
Craving attention
I wore my push up bra to flex
with a short skirt right below my little ass
Even if my mother would've raised me, she couldn't teach me
class
And when she put that one nigga in front of me

17

DYAMOND IN THE ROUGH

She left the door open for other niggaz to trespass
DONE.

That poem said it all.

I moved back to Los Angeles in 2003 after spending a year with my dad in Texas, to find my mom engaged to some man. From the day I met him, I knew I didn't like him. He was a know it all and always had something smart to say. He even laughed at his own jokes; he was a real cornball. The whole family couldn't see through him, but I did. One day I told my mom I hated him, and she washed my mouth out with soap. I was 9 years old when my mother married this man and I cried my eyes out to my grandma in the next hotel room. In the fourth grade, we moved out of grandma's house in View Park and moved to Inglewood. Things only got worse. My step father and I argued every other day. They even started waking me— a 4th grader, up at 3 or 4 in the morning to wash the dishes and to mop the kitchen floor. Something to this day, I still don't know how to do. I remember one day I was starving and my mom yelled that the food was ready, when I came downstairs I picked up a plate and she asked me "WHAT THE FUCK ARE YOU DOING?", then made me put my plate back and told me that "the man of the house eats first". They both worked early mornings but always came home at night. One evening I walked into my mother's room to ask her a question and her husband was underneath the cover eating her out and she had the nerve to hold a conversation with me like it was nothing. I walked away in disgust and filled with anger.

Sometime after that, I came home from school like any other day. I walked through the front door and the first thing I saw was him sitting on the couch. I looked at him like I hated him. I cut my eyes so hard, before I could open them my mother had me pinned up against our wooden door with her forearm against my small throat. I started choking from having the wind knocked out of me, so I started spitting up. I remember my mom yelling at me "If you throw up, Ima make your clean it up with your mouth". I tried my hardest to catch my breath and to calm down until I could stop gagging. My stepdad called me over to the couch where he and my

18

mother sat to tell me "Your mother will always put me before you" and my mother just sat there in silence.

I turned to her and started screaming and hyperventilating with big tears rushing down my face. I always thought my mother was the most beautiful woman in the world, but after that day it was *FUCK THAT BITCH*. Later that night when my step dad got in the shower, my mother came into my room and sat on my bed. I asked her if what he said was true and she whispered no.

However, the damage was already done. After that night, nothing would be the same not even between them because I watched both of them start cheating on each other right in front of my own eyes. Months later, I graduated from the 5th grade and my mother told me I had to move in with Brandee and Auntie BJ. I was so happy to get away from the both of them, I never even asked why I had to move in with Brandee. Shortly after I did, I saw why I had when I turned on the news. My mom and her husband had been charged with embezzlement.

It was the summer before 6th grade that I lost my virginity. I was 12 years old and the boy was 16. My older cousin Adriana was there but never stopped me and by all means, it wasn't her fault that I was lost. I take full responsibility for everything I did, but I'm sure I could've had a little guidance somewhere along the line. Looking back, she probably was just as lost as me.

When I moved into Brandee's, I realized I wasn't the only one who was boy crazy. Brandee was more boy crazy than me. We stayed up all night long talking to niggaz on the partyline. We'd talk on the phone with niggaz we knew and niggaz we'd never even met. We had Myspace profiles even when I wasn't allowed to have one. When my mom found out she was pissed and tried to come over and beat my ass with a belt, but Auntie BJ told her she wasn't gonna hit me while I lived in her house.

Eventually my mother just stopped coming over and stopped calling then I really thought *fuck that bitch*.

Sooner than later, Brandee and I started to go to Melvin's football practice when he played for the Inglewood Jets. We went religiously just to flirt with all the football players. Thirsty little girl. I figured if I couldn't get the love from my parents, I would get it from a nigga off the street, just like the romances I watched in movies.

I wrote this poem called LONELY 101, another piece to my puzzle.

LONELY 101

I feel so lonely let me text every nigga but mine
Let me act out slutty so every nigga but mine will acknowledge
I'm fine
Attention is what I need but I want him to want me and only
me
I want him to respond to my text on time
Especially since he's truly the only one on my mind
All the I Love Yous will never make up for all the lonely times
I feel so lonely
but I'm not about to bug you
What for
When I can just go to any other nigga
if I'm really craving attention or more
I feel so lonely
I should act out like a whore and knock on every door but
yours
Scared you don't want me there because you never took the
time to make me feel assured
I feel so lonely
I don't want to call just to get ignored
My biggest fear is rejection, all my life I felt neglected
Do you hear me crying out or are you just staring at all my
missed calls?
Not to worry all your homeboys know the protocol
No
No
No
Thank you Conscious for stepping in
Tell me something
Where the fuck have you been?
Why the fuck did you almost let misogyny come within?

You know he likes to trick us lonely women into committing
sins
DONE.

In the middle of 7th grade I moved back to Texas. It was January and after going to a new school for a couple months I made a new friend. I ended up spending the night at her house one weekend and that weekend I had intercourse with her cousin. Eight months later, when we were in the 8th grade one of Taylor's friends came over and I had intercourse with him. You asked me if we used a condom and I lied and said yes.

Fast forward to the middle of freshman year when I was 15, I wanted to go to the gynecologist because I felt like I had something. I told you I thought it was a yeast infection, but I knew it was more. I just didn't feel like hiding it from you anymore. When the doctor office called saying I had chlamydia I watched you grow so angry that you threw the house phone across the kitchen. At that moment, every heartache I've ever felt came rushing towards me. Flashbacks after flashbacks replayed and I suddenly became angry and defensive.

No one really understands why I truly hate my mom and it's because she left me hanging in this wild ass world, clueless and thirsty. See I wanted to be like my mother, but colder and I moved out here with that mentality. Not even realizing that I hated her so much that I allowed the hatred to consume my body to the point of hating myself. I chased after boys and got my ass caught up at only 14.

Lately, I've been told that I'm looking awfully skinny and I noticed a few months ago that not only have I lost color but have patches all over my skin. My migraines have been terrible, and I have sores inside my mouth. Since the beginning of sophomore year, the thought of having HIV has haunted me every single day. But the more you love me, the harder I love you. Your cancer had been getting worse sophomore year and that's when I told myself I would wait until I was 18 to go get tested because this wasn't anybody's problem but mine. My guilty conscious has harassed me so much that I feel like I am a demon. I know something is truly wrong with me because as you read, sex has always been in me ever since I was a little girl. The most recent cuts on my body are from me punishing myself for being promiscuous.

After living here with you, Taylor, and Josh I realized that I was loved— but it was too late. I had already made those two mistakes with those two boys. I'm telling you now because I don't want to hurt you anymore than I already have. I tried to convince myself that it would be selfless of me to not bother you with this, but I've become so depressed that I've been cutting non-stop, wanting to kill myself every other day. I just don't because I know that would be so much more selfish and not fair to you because you fight your battle every day to stay alive for us.

PLEASE DON'T JUDGE ME
:(I'M SORRY
I just want to get tested.

I take full responsibility for all my actions that boil down to me being a lonely girl searching for love in all the wrong places.

I'M SORRY AND I LOVE YOU.

**-your niece, your daughter, your best friend
Dyamond.**

DYAMOND IN THE ROUGH GUIDANCE CENTER
PROGRESS NOTE
Dyamond Taylor
Session #1

DOB:11/3/94
SEX: F
Appt. Date: 6/8/11
Start Time: 1:30pm

Description of session, including behavioral observations and response to treatment:
Pt is a return client of this thx. Pt presented very depressed and tired. Pt was adopted by her aunt. She does refer to aunt as "mom. Pt's Mo explained that a few weeks ago she got a letter from pt explaining that pt had made mistakes. Mo was very tearful as she explained that pt told her she feels there's no point of living. She said she does not want to be a problem for anyone. She said she feels she knows the reason for having sex and trying to feel accepted since she feels rejected by bio Mo. However, pt did acknowledge that her not being here would hurt her family, especially her grandmother who took care of her as a young child and whom she is very close to. Pt's Mo/aunt has battled cancer since December 2007. Pt denied SI/HI. She agreed to continue with therapy despite hesitation and "not knowing how this will help."

Assessment of progress in treatment and current functioning:
Pt has regressed to being very depressed.
She was engaged and cooperative but hesitant to returning to counseling.

Stop Time: 2:05pm

23

DYAMOND IN THE ROUGH

DYAMOND IN THE ROUGH GUIDANCE CENTER

Dyamond Taylor
DOB: 11/3/94
Sex: F

PROGRESS NOTE

Session #: 2
Appt. Date: 6/16/11
Start Time: 11:00am

Description of session, including behavioral obeservations and response to treatment:
Pt's mood was euthymic with congruent affect. She smiled and laughed for session. She said she did tell a few friends about her fear of having HIV/AIDS and no one had a negative reaction. She said they were positive and supportive. Pt was engaged and initiated conversations about family and peer relationships. She was also able to acknowledge that people love her and want her to be a part of their life.

Pt also talked about her dream of having a daughter one day.

Assessment of progress in treatment and current functioning:
Pt's mood was stable and her anxiety has decreased she was able to have more rational thoughts.

Dyamond

DYAMOND IN THE ROUGH GUIDANCE CENTER

Dyamond Taylor
DOB: 11/3/94
Sex: F

PROGRESS NOTE

Session #: 5
Appt. Date: 7/28/11
Start Time: 2:00pm

Description of session, including behavioral observations and response to treatment:
Pt's aunt called thx day before session. (7/27/11).
Aunt reported pt's HIV test was negative.
Aunt also addressed the concerns about pt being depressed and staying her room.
At time of session, her cousin (17y/o Taylor Hall) joined session. Cousin said that pt is "alone". Pt was more open and expressive about her negative, irrational thoughts, irritability and thoughts of cutting herself. She denied SI/HI. Pt said she stays to herself at home or talks to cousin. Pt expressed that she is angry and knows her depression is from her "past". Pt was able to process her anger at bio parents, aunt, and others in her life who are "fake and judgmental." Pt agreed to safety plan of coming to session each week and having psychiatric evaluation. Pt will be out of town in CA next week.

Assessment of progress in treatment and current functioning:
Pt cried in session and process her depression. She denied SI/HI and agreed to psychiatric evaluation .

DYAMOND IN THE ROUGH

April 6th, 2011

Dear Dyamond,
You have really grown, keep it up.
Remember to be a Lady first.
I hope you find what you really want to do in life, because you
will do great at it.
I wish I was there to help, but I believe I taught you the basics.
You are a Diamond!

I hope we had enough good times so you can remember.
Put God first and everything will fall in place.
I love you!
Love
Mom/Aunt Nikki

April 6 2001
~~March 4 2011~~

Dear Dyamond.

You have Really grown, keep
It up Remember To be a Lady First
I hope you fine what you Really want
To do In Life, Because you will Great
At It I wish I was There To To
help but I believe I Tought you
The Basic. you are a Diamond

I hope we had ~~sen~~ enough
good Times so you can Remember
Put God first and everything ~~will~~
Will fail In Place. I Love you!

Love
Mom/Aunt Nikki

DYAMOND IN THE ROUGH

DYAMOND IN THE ROUGH GUIDANCE CENTER

Dyamond Taylor
DOB: 11/3/94
Sex: F

PROGRESS NOTE

Session #13

Appt. Date: 1/24/12

Start Time: 2:00pm

Description of session, including behavioral obeservations and response to treatment:

Pt was very calm. Thx asked how she was doing and she told thx that her adoptive
Mo/aunt passed away 1/20/12.
Pt expressed being confused and still being in shock.
She gave me factual details about the last month of her Mo's life. She also explained how she found out
and reaction of family.
Pt's processing was factual.

Assessment of progress in treatment and current functioning:
Pt was calm and appeared to be in shock since Mo's death on 1/20/12

Stop Time: 2:50pm

Jina's *Pregnant*

I've always loved when you told me this story. It was April 1994, when you'd just given birth to Taylor. You were filled with pure happiness and there was nothing that could ruin your mood. Uncle Joey was at the hospital, along with your mother, and of course, my dad showed up to show you and his newborn nephew all the love.

You were my dad's big sister and he was your little brother who you loved so dearly. Y'all grew up together very tight, y'all were each other's best friends. He didn't know when the right time would be, but he had something to tell you. Nervously he announced "Jina's pregnant". You were pissed. Bad timing? You told me you were mad at him all the way up until my mother gave birth to me.

But, from that day on, there wasn't anything your kids had, that I didn't. You made sure I had everything your sons did, from sending me to Page Private School to buying me my first pink electric Barbie Jeep. You made sure I had a roof over my head, even when I didn't live with you. I'd come to visit you in the summer, and you made sure I always had my own room at your house. You made sure I had enough school clothes, even called at the end of summer to ask my mother if I needed anything.

You always loved me equally to your children and as I got older, I always told you thank you, but since you've passed, I've dwelled on whether I really *showed* you.

For Granted

You were diagnosed with cancer in October 2007
and asked me to come live with you in January 2008.
Even after people insisted that I would be too much for you,
You didn't care.
I was the daughter you always dreamed of having.
You boasted and bragged about me to your co-workers and
friends.
You acknowledged that I'd been through some shit
and still took on the challenge of having to raise your own two
kids plus a broken one.
You scolded me over the small things to protect me
while I was only hard headed and heavily guarded.
Your stern ways and structured love overwhelmed me
because I wasn't used to having anything like it.
I fought you with my attitude
and you fought back with pure love.
You never ever gave up on me
but stressed to me that if I didn't change my attitude for the
better
nothing good in life would come to me.
You made it clear you'd love me through thick and thin and
forgave me for the mistakes I made.
You kept my secrets and even told me yours.
You loved me when my parents weren't capable
and I still took you for granted.

One Day

There isn't one day that goes by where I don't think of you
and now I feel deranged because I lost you when I had you.
I was your daughter and best friend.
I was
your
Fuckin'
In-Home Nurse.
I tried my best to do everything right.
Spent long days at chemotherapy with you.
Spent many school nights in the hospital with you.
Made sure you took your medicine on time,
every morning and every night.

I never seen such roles
switched
the way God played it.

You saved me
but I couldn't save you.

So blind to the fact that You were my angel on earth,
I now have to accept the fact that you're an angel in the sky
who is watching over me.

CHAPTER 3

Blood Dyamonds
Are Mined in Warzones

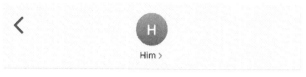

Him ›

iMessage
Today 2:42 PM

Is it crazy that till this day I can't stop thinking about your love? I still have a box full of pictures and poems you wrote me that I still read.

7
Years Old

I remember the day my parents sat me down and asked me if I wanted them to be together. I told them no. They asked me why not, and I told them because they fought too much. Well, they broke up after that and I blamed myself.

After all these years, I can remember just a few of their many fights. So, bear with me as I start to tell you the first one.

In the poem *Young Hoe,* I wrote, "Ever since I was a little girl, all I ever knew about was sex/ I guess my parents sexing in front of my innocent eyes was never a threat". But that story didn't end there. After waking up in the first place because I was thirsty, I turned over to my parent's bed and they were fucking. I immediately felt some weird sort of sensation in my premature private part. I don't remember how old I was exactly, but I do remember the scene of them fucking because I remember the cable box light shining bright and having to force myself back to sleep with all the noise.

Here's where the story picks up, I woke back up again that same night, however this time it was from the sound of them arguing. At one point I was able to remember the exact conversations I heard them having, but I can't remember anymore. I only remember them both being ass naked with my mom crying and yelling at him.

The next fight I remember; they woke me out my sleep again. It was the night or early morning of 4th of July and my dad came home late. I remember waking up to my mom screaming going off about scratches on his back? Asking him why he had them when she started hitting him, I can remember him throwing her on me while I was lying in their bed. When I started screaming and crying, he left. He just fucking left us in the bed crying. She was crying because she was hurt, and I was crying because I was scared. This was the first night I had ever stayed awake and saw the sun come up. While my mom cried herself to sleep, I watched Tom & Jerry waiting for my dad to come back.

Another day, another time I remember walking to our bedroom, and I could feel that something was wrong. My dad had his back to the doorway, and he was sitting on the edge of the bed facing our bedroom window. He wouldn't look at me at first, but I made him turn my way with my sweet voice. When he finally did look at me, we were practically nose to nose. I watched tears fall from my father's eyes and it scared the shit out of my little ass. I had never in my life seen my father so broken to the point where he was crying. His energy was so scary that I started crying with him.

When my mom walked in the room, he gave her the ugliest, dirtiest look. He looked at her with pure hate in his eyes, and it was almost like his energy transferred to my little body because I thought to myself "I hate her". While trying to ask my dad what was wrong, he sat there in silence with tears falling down his face. I never saw him in so much pain, hurt.

The last fight I can recall is when my dad bought my mom some ring. He told me he was trying to propose, but she told me he wasn't. All I remember is him throwing the ring at her and her crying, calling me in the room to tell me "Baby!!! Your daddy just called me a hoe." My response was very clear, a confused as fuck seven-year old I asked, "Like the water hose?" and all she said was "No, it's a bad word". Her cry became even more hysterical. I got scared and went to my grandma and grandpa's stairs and started screaming for them. My grandpa came down the stairs with his police baton and told my dad "Damon, you gotta leave." I remember crying, as I watched my dad walk out that door.

Even though those are the only fights I can remember, I have too many flashbacks of my younger self full of fear, running to my grandparent's stairs crying out for help because my parents were fighting. It turned into my first instinct after a while. Each time my grandpa would come down the stairs with either his police baton or shotgun. He'd always tell my dad calmly "Damon, you got to go".

Each time my dad would leave, he'd always find a way to sneak back in. My grandma would knock on our bedroom door, and my dad would jump up and hide in our closet. My grandma would yell "DAMON BETTER NOT BE IN THERE" until my mom would open the door. She would never see him either. Thirty minutes later I'd watch my dad climb out our bedroom window to ring the front doorbell to come inside and do the exact same shit he'd been doing.

Except that one day when they sat me down and asked me "Dyamond, do you want us to be together?" or maybe it was "Dyamond, do you think we should be together?". I just remember the courage I had to tell them no. Shortly after I remember no longer having to run to my grandparent's stairs. I remember no longer seeing my mom or dad cry ever again. I remember no longer seeing my dad sneak out our bedroom window. I barely remember seeing my dad at all. And I blamed it all on myself. Traumatized and torn, I didn't know what either of those feelings was.

**I was just 7 motherfucking years old
and this was my example of love.**

TEENAGE FEVER

I packed an extra small sparkly two-piece bikini that I never would've worn in front of my aunt. She dropped me off at my friend's house for a sleepover; sleeping was the last thing I had in mind. My titties were barely covered, while the whole bottom of my ass hung out. I knew what I was doing when my homegirl told me she was throwing a pool party. I'd been living in Texas for two and a half years at this point and never knew what I was really missing out on until I met my homegirl. She was older than me; known for having all the niggaz and I was too excited because they'd all be there. With that bathing suit, I knew I would get some of those niggaz.

I met *him* there, but we didn't talk much. His best friend quickly grabbed my attention and I can't even lie I was mesmerized by a couple niggaz that night. While I didn't show it, I was dying of thirst and even with all the niggaz there I somehow ended up kissing a girl at the end of the night.

I kept in contact with his best friend through Facebook. We'll call him Benny. We would chat and flirt, I guess you could say I had a crush. Benny was tall, had dark sexy skin, extremely athletic body, and was a star football player at his school. I found Benny very charismatic and charming to say the least. When the summer ended, I tried to shoot my shot by asking him to be my homecoming date, but he politely declined because of my age. I couldn't do anything but feel rejected and front like I respected it.

I went to a teen club that next weekend with my friends and ran into the same *boy* I didn't care too much for at the pool party. When *he* saw me, I smiled and gave *him* a hug. Soon I found *him* in front of me and my friends every other song. I started to notice that *he* too was tall and actually really handsome. Truthfully, I'd never seen a face like *his* before. Then again, I never bothered to pay attention to *him* until that night. Towards the end of the night, the DJ decided to slow it down and play "Slow Dance" by Miss Keri Baby. I started feeling myself and of course, *he* somehow ended up right behind me. Grinding to the beat of the song, our bodies synchronized as soon as the second verse came on all the way until the end of the bridge. Our chemistry was undeniable.

Before I got into my ride's car that night, I walked with *him* over to his homeboy's car and continued to do a little flirting until we exchanged numbers. Sooner than later our "get to know you" phase started. *He* asked me how old I was, and I told *him* I was 15. When I asked *him his* age, *he* told me *he* was 19. I felt *his* energy become skeptical, so I tried to make *him* feel better by telling *him* I'd be 16 in two months. *He* told me I acted way more mature than my age and seemed relieved. *He* was too attracted to me to back out. We'd talk all day, every day, and all fucking night. Getting to know each other in and out, sharing stories, and I made *him* laugh all night. *He's* was a cancer, so *he* had a way of making me feel like I was the most gorgeous girl *he'd* been with and after seeing a picture of *his* ex-girlfriend, I can say I was.

We'd start going on dates to football games, where *he* met the rest of my friends and I met all of *his*. *He* had one friend who took a strong liking to me immediately. *He* told me that they were so close they were more like brothers. That same friend would go on to tell *him* how much he liked me and that *he* should make me *his* girlfriend. I saw him at every football game we went, to the point where he ended up becoming my friend.

Days after I turned 16, this same friend *he* called *his* brother got shot in the head and passed away. *He* was so devastated and young; I don't even think *he* knew how to handle his friend's death. It was a hard thing for me to even talk about with *him* because it didn't feel like my place.

I showed up to the funeral to pay my respects or maybe to just be able to see *him* outside of a football game. I didn't see *him* until the end, but when I did find *him,* I couldn't fucking wait. I saw very clear from a distance that *he* was hurt. I walked up to *him* and opened my arms. While I wrapped my arms around *him* tightly, I could feel *him* let go. *He* found the comfort *he* needed in me too and cried on my left shoulder while *he* buried *his* face in my neck.

Since I didn't see *him* until the end, I stayed out longer than what I was supposed to. I just wanted *him* to see and feel that I was there for *him* because I needed him to know that's what I planned on doing from that point on. That night happened to be a weeknight and I had school in the morning. When I finally walked into my

39

house, my Aunt Nikki was furious. She told me I didn't even know the boy and even though I got in trouble I didn't care. *He* was worth it to me.

Naïve

After that night, our bond grew stronger and we became official. Christmas came around, and I was head over heels for *him*. *He* just became dreamier than ever before. We were so into each other that we'd still hadn't experienced our first argument. I was already daydreaming of my future with him. Fantasies about how many kids we were going to have, what names we'd pick for them. For the first time, I was in love. *He* came over to my house and met my Aunt Nikki and even she loved *him*. *He'd* spoil me and I spoil *him* back. I remember opening the Christmas gift *he* bought me. It was this beautiful Hello Kitty watch. I loved it and I loved *him*. *He* gave me a happiness I'd never felt before. Everything was going perfect. I was so in love with *him*, that I was obsessed.

When we weren't together, I'd look at pictures of *him*. Weeks went by, and I was on Facebook like any other day. I found myself on *his* page, and I just decided to look at *his* tagged photos. I saw a picture of *him* and another girl who almost looked similar to me.. but could never. They took the picture in the store that I knew *he* bought my watch in. I immediately felt angry and turned very territorial. When I brought it up to *him, he* told me she was a friend that lived in another state and that she helped *him* pick out my watch. I believed *him* because I loved him, and I knew that *he* loved me.

I was still 16 years old when I asked my Aunt Nikki if I could go to sleep over my friend Baby Aubri's house. My aunt didn't really let me go to people's houses, and she definitely didn't let me get in the car with just anybody. But she let me go to Aubri's that night, and even though that's what I said I was doing, it wasn't. I really went to a house party with Baby Aubri and ended up leaving with *him*.

After the party, *he* took me to *his* car and drove us up the street to *his* house. This would be the first time we ever had intercourse. *He* laid me on *his* bed and asked me if I was sure I wanted to do it. *He* was so special to me, that I decided to give *him* all of me.

INSECURE

Sooner than later, I guess my Aunt Nikki's car ride rule got old to the nigga because *he* ended up cheating on me with that same girl as soon as she moved here. *He* cheated on me for... I don't know, a year, with the same old girl. I knew she wasn't better than me, she just had more freedom than I did. So, *he* liked her just as much. I was heartbroken because it got to the point where *he* started openly cheating on me for the world to see. It was plain and simple that she was plain and simple. An off-brand version of me. I was Chanel and she was Charlotte Russe. We both were just yella girls with big curly hair and after a while, my self-esteem no longer felt present. I just wanted to set her fucking hair on fire.

I had first cut myself towards the end of my freshman year because I was mad I was even in fucking Texas. I was so angry at my parents for abandoning me, but once this nigga started blatantly cheating on me and forever lying about it, I just started taking out my anger and pain on myself. Cutting myself when I knew *he* was with her, cutting myself when I knew *he* was lying to me. One day my uncle saw my arm and took me to see a therapist. Shortly after that session, my uncle had forbid me to see my boyfriend because "it wasn't healthy for me to be with *him*". But once I stopped seeing *him*, I grew even sadder and my cutting would ultimately continue in the worse way.

DYING OF THIRST

I was sadder than I'd ever been, but I continued to live my "normal" teenage life. My best friend Sasha and I went to a graduation party by our school. This was my first time ever getting drunk, Sasha and I drank an entire can of grape Four Loko each. Ghetto, I know. Anyways, I had gotten really drunk and even though this was a graduation party by our school, it also happens to be one of *his* friends. When I saw *him* walk in the party, I immediately got emotional. I turned to Sasha and one of *his* friends and told them I wanted to die. *He* walked right past me and didn't even speak. I couldn't take being ignored. I was intoxicated and in so much pain, I didn't care to hide it. I tried to jump off a cliff in this gorgeous backyard. When I felt my body just about to go free, I no longer felt heartbreak. I couldn't feel anything. But that got interrupted by Sasha's screaming while she and *his* fat ass friend snatched me from falling.

Somehow weeks later *he* found his way back in my life and as much as my hopes went up, it didn't take much for *him* to hurt me again. I can still hear Sasha's cries, as she tried to break down her bathroom door while I sat in there slowly cutting into my arm. Finally, she got me out and cried more. Shit, I cried with her. After that, I decided I wouldn't cut myself anymore.

DYAMOND IN THE ROUGH GUIDANCE CENTER
Dyamond Taylor
DOB: 11/3/94
Sex: F

Date: 2011

PROGRESS NOTE   Session #: 8

Description of session, including behavioral obeservations and response to treatment:

Pt admitted she is "never happy." Pt said that she wants to have a relationship with boyfriend, despite her aunt and uncle telling her the "relationship is unhealthy." Pt asked thx to help her explain to her uncle how she feels about boyfriend. Pt repeatedly got upset when talking about bio parents. She described her boyfriend as "fun, listener, and makes her laugh." Pt said she is not "attached " to him forever bu wants the relationship right now. Pt and thx role played her explaining her views about bio parents and boyfriend to her uncle.

Assessment of progress in treatment and current functioning:
Pt was able to conclude that her irritability is from her past and aunt pushing relationship with her bio parents. She was very insightful ad thoughts were logical. Pt denied self harm thoughts or behaviors.

CURIOSITY

A whole lot of time passed, and *he* seemed ready to be with me. At least so I thought because we didn't last on good terms for long. We'd broken up by homecoming because when I asked *him* to come to my homecoming football game, *he* told me *he* was too old. And by the time *he* felt bad enough to tell me *he* changed *his* mind, I had already invited someone else. He sent a text that said, "Since you wanna act single, be single" and I replied with the driest "OK". I was just over it by this time. Plus, in the midst of all our on and offs, I had started talking to other people.

Truth be told the nigga I invited, I had dated during my freshman year. And while I never fucked him during my freshman year, he cheated on my ass too, with an ugly ass boogawulf (google it). But I still managed to be cool with him and while he was the same age as my boyfriend, I didn't have to beg him to come because he loved football and his high school alma mater was my school's rival. I didn't have any intentions to fuck him, but I did the week after the football game.

After that is when the fun really begun, I got my very first car in November when I turned 17. Only thing was, my aunt started getting sicker and sicker, so she stayed in the hospital for weeks at a time. That's when I found time to explore my sexuality, how I wanted to. For every person fucked, I found myself no longer caring or missing my ex. When I thought I was starting to have the most fun, reality shortly ended that.

INTUITION

Thanksgiving came and my ex showed up to my house because Sasha was talking to one of his homeboys, so they both came. We talked, laughed, made out, and shit. *He* even asked if I could spend the night that night, but I told *him* I couldn't because I had to give my aunt her meds in the morning. To make him feel better, I offered to come over and cook breakfast for *him* and *his* friends once I had taken care of my aunt. When it was time for him to leave, *he* told me to come to his house at 10 a.m., then kissed me, and left. When Sasha and I got ready to go to sleep I told her we

44

would go to the grocery store before we went to *his* house and that we would go at 9 instead of 10 because I wanted to see what hoe *he*'d have over there.

The next morning, I gave my aunt her meds, left to the grocery store then headed to *his* side of town. When we pulled up, I parked my car and knocked on *his* front door. His homeboy came outside and closed the door behind him real fast. *He* looked at me with this dumb ass smile on *his* face and said, "Let's go to the grocery store" and I said, "Nah, we already went. Open up the fucking door." When I turned around, I seen the girl's raggedy car in the driveway with a Hello Kitty decal on her window. So, I then asked everyone to come outside, but instead, my ex only came out and pulled her car up on *his* front lawn. I was shocked. I had never seen no pussy shit like this before. Immediately filled with anger, I watched her walk out *his* front door and get straight in her car, all while this nigga's homeboy was bear hugging me. Kicking my legs hard as fuck, I tried my hardest to get free from him, but he was stronger than me. She drove off and my ex drove off in *his* own car pretending as if *he* had somewhere to be.

I lost my shit completely. I took out the carton of eggs from my trunk and threw every one of them at *his* fucking house. Sasha moved to *his* dad's truck and threw the gallon of orange juice all over it. To finish it, I walked up to *his* full trash bins and knocked them all over until they were empty.

When *he* pulled back up to *his* house, he let me in and I cooked what food *he* had in *his* fridge. I offered *him* a plate, but *he* was so mad *he* didn't want to eat. I didn't care, I saw it for what it was and got my anger out as best as I could. So, I ate while Sasha was upstairs losing her virginity. I was still there when *his* parents walked in with concerned looks on their faces and asked him "Somebody egged our house?" I replied with an "Mhmm" all while giving them both hugs and kisses. Sasha walked down the stairs shortly after, and we left. After that day, I didn't talk to *him* anymore. I was done.

25

FEAR

Christmas break came and I pulled up to the homegirl house. Sure enough, I ran into his best friend Benny. The same best friend I had my eyes on at the pool party when I was only 15 years old. He'd only gotten finer. I ran into him two days later, at the same place. This time wasn't too many people and we chilled in the studio vibing with each other. We had a lot of things in common, but the most important thing was poetry. When we spoke to each other, it was like every word off our tongues was poetry.

A week later he invited me to his dorm room, so I went. When I walked in, I felt nervous for some reason. We chilled and talked for a couple of hours until we started kissing. When I felt Benny unbuckle my jeans, I suddenly felt like I had to throw up. I tried to tell him no and to stop, but he was so overzealous I guess he didn't think I was really serious. It was like I just couldn't get my ex's face out my fucking head. When his best friend got up to turn off his dorm room light, I panicked and ran to the opposite corner of the room. He managed to grab me and put me on his bed. When he started pulling my pants down, I started to cry, and he finally stopped. He looked at me and said he was sorry. I told him I wanted to leave so he opened his door to let me out.

When I got to the parking lot, I ran to my car and couldn't help but let out all of my tears. Not only was I fucking terrified, I realized I was still in love with my ex and was about to do something I would regret. A couple of weeks went by and I still hadn't talked to my ex. When *he* did finally hit me up, I was still so spooked that I just told *him*. I told *him* everything.

BROKEN

He ended up texting me again a few days later to see if I was okay because *he* heard about the girl and her friends pulling up to my school. Let me remind you, I'm the only one in high school in this whole love triangle. So, *he* asked me what happened, and I began to tell *him*:

After my last class, I walked out to my car and seen that bitch same raggedy ass hello kitty decal parked in the next spot waiting for me. As I got closer, I counted four heads. When I opened the door to my car, I looked at them and asked what was up. They told me they wanted to fight, so I told them to follow my car. For some reason, they had these shocked ass looks on their faces.

I took them to some apartments by my school and stepped out of my car. When everybody was finally done talking, the girl said "she didn't want to fight anymore" so I fought one of her best friends. When we finished, I told all them bitches I rather go through this than get my heart broke and I meant that shit.

When I got home, I was late yet again. My Aunt Nikki was so ruthless by this time, her illness had her saying anything. She was pissed. I told her I got into a fight and she didn't even ask for any details. She just told me I was stupid for fighting over a nigga. I was so hurt when she said that, I ran upstairs to my bathroom and sliced my arms and legs up. Never did I fight over a nigga! Them grown bitches pulled up to my high school wanting to fight me. I had no one with me, but still had the courage to fight them.

Whether it would have been one or four. I got out there and handled that shit by myself, just to come home and be called stupid. I was already hurt I had to fight in the first place. My aunt made it no better. No comfort, no compassion. If I knew it was her disease talking, I probably wouldn't have cut myself up the way I did. I blame the cancer.

ENVY

Weeks after me and *him* cleared the air, he asked me if *he* could come over that next day. I told *him* to just come that Friday. When *he* called me that day, I was crying hysterically and I told *him, he* couldn't come over. *He* asked me why not and I told *him* that my aunt had died.

A couple of days before my aunt's funeral, *he* put me on three-way with the knock off girl and I muted my phone. She was going off, crying, about how *he* had some bitch sleeping on "her side of the bed". I felt bad for her because I knew exactly how she felt. At the end of the phone call, I listened close, while *he* broke things off with her ass for good.

47

He showed up at my aunt's funeral days later and gave me the same comfort I had once given *him*. After that night, we became exclusive. We'd be together every day as soon as I got out of class. If *he* wasn't at my house, I was at *his*. We practically started living together. When we finally felt like what seemed to be at our peak, *he* was all about me. I knew *he* only cared about me. I knew *he* stopped seeing the girl, but it was me who kept seeing her ass.

She just couldn't stop harassing me. She was obsessed. She started texting me with these threats, using sentences that sounded too familiar. She sent me lines of my very own poetry and I couldn't understand how she even got ahold of it. Until one day, she sent me "Confessions of a Lonely Girl", then it clicked to me. At the time I sent that personal email to my aunt, I forwarded it to my boyfriend because I thought *he* deserved to know as well. I trusted *him* that much, while *he* trusted that bitch with *his* whole email password. Ain't that bout a bitch?

After being threatened and blackmailed so many times, I decided to put the email out on my Tumblr blog my damn self and even went the extra mile to tell everybody about her trying to bully and expose me. I expressed on my blog that if I didn't have the strength and courage to put out this email myself, I would've probably killed myself. This little bitch had put me through so much, I woke up one day and thought fuck it. I shaved my whole head bald. I didn't want to see big curly hair no fucking more.

SPITE

Months went by when I finally thought that me and *him* were the happiest, but soon my happiness started to fade. *He* started to lack ambition and I became eager to find myself. We just started growing apart. I broke up with *him* and I told *him* I'd come back if he'd let me.

As months passed, I found myself at his best friend Benny's house. There was just something about this nigga, that even after the first encounter I still went back. I just had to find out for myself and my lust was in full effect. Each time I spent with him, he'd talk more and more shit about my ex. So, I just assume that they weren't cool anymore or at least that this nigga wasn't a real friend anyways. I pulled up one night and put it on him. I didn't let him do anything he wanted to either. I fucked him so hard I broke his bed. I took all my frustrations out on him.

When I was finished, I suggested we played a game, "it's called Confessions, you have to tell me your biggest secret" and he did... he really fucking did. Aha. I was long gone and disgusted the next day. I couldn't help but to feel heartless. I didn't know what was wrong with me. I just knew I didn't really care about the nigga.

MANIPULATION

. The more he kept telling me not to tell my ex, I knew I had to be the one to tell *him* first because something told me this nigga was going twist the truth and manipulate the situation. Ironically, (not really) we both texted *him* at the same time, but my ex was too hurt to hear anything I said past my first sentence. I didn't even get a chance to twist the truth. I had simply texted "I fucked up" and *he* already knew what I was talking about. He then took his pain to twitter and blasted me so *him* and *his* friends could call me all types of hoes and sluts.

A month passed, when a green snake emoji appeared on my phone screen. It was Benny texting me how terrible he felt, you know yada-yada. I read his ass for filth, and after he asked me if I would come over so he could talk to both me and my ex.

So there we were, all three of us on the couch with me in the middle. When Benny finally broke the silence, he looked at my ex and said, "I lied to you". He told him everything. From how he really lured me in and even professed the envy he felt towards *him*. When I glanced over at my ex, *he* looked like *he* wanted to slap the fuck out this nigga. Benny finished his apology and I left. I really only came for my ex to hear the whole truth.

DAMAGED

Shortly after, we got back together. Time past as we worked hard on rebuilding our relationship, but I still felt like I was missing something. One day, *he* was sitting in my room and after keeping it in so long, I told *him* I was having second thoughts about us being together.

When I was done, *he* had *his* head buried in *his* hands for ten minutes. When I tried to get *him* to talk to me, the ten minutes turned into twenty minutes. *He*'d completely shut down. I begged *him* to talk to me until I reached a point where I could no longer take *his* silence anymore, and I lost it. I started socking *him* in *his* back repeatedly; yelling at *him* to look at me.

When *he* finally decided to look up at me, I could see tears falling down *his* cheeks. *He*'d been crying that whole time and at that moment I had a flashback of my 7-year-old self-seeing my father cry for the first time. I had the same little 7-year-old feelings take over my body. I was scared, but this time instead of feeling like I hated my mom... I hated myself. Seeing *him* cry broke me down to the point where I started crying.

After that, *he* started stroking my head until we both fell asleep as if nothing ever happened. But something did happen.

I opened the door to what would be the cycle of abuse *he* watched *his* own parents go through. In the beginning of our relationship, he confided in me that *he* once read in *his* mother's diary about *his* father abusing her. I could see that the resentment *he* had towards *his* father as a teenager had carried over presently. Somehow that all went out the window the night I went crazy and started socking *him* repeatedly.

I was so young, I wasn't aware of what I had done. Little did I know what I was in for, but I was about to find out. I felt all our memories filled with pure love quickly fade as our last days ended extremely dark.

TOXICITY

I remember us having dinner at his parents' house on a night that seemed normal but as we got ready to leave, I saw that *he*'d been texting one of my good friends. Once I decided to question *him*, he immediately got defensive and while driving us home, I told *him* I didn't want *him* texting her anymore. In which *he* flat out said no and out of anger, I asked *him* if *he* wanted me to fuck another one of *his* best friends. Before *he* could even respond, I just felt my head smashed into my driver's window. In that moment, I let go of the wheel to fight *him*. All I can remember after that is the food that was in *his* lap– all over my seats and floor. Not too long after the first incident, I was laying in his bed when he said something to me that made me kick *his* head right into the wall. *He* got up and slammed my little ass on the ground.

Another time I can't forget is when I came over to his house on one of my lunch breaks to talk, and of course we ended up arguing. Desperate to leave, I looked at the time to try and tell *him* I had to be back at school. When I started walking out the door, he was right behind me. He tried pulling me back in as he slammed a wooden door closed on half of my body. When I screamed, *he* told me that I wasn't leaving until we figured shit out. I told *him* whatever *he* wanted to hear.

Weeks after that, we were leaving my house to get food when we started arguing and before we could even get all the way out of my neighborhood, *he* again smashed my head against the window. This time he held it there with all *his* might so that I couldn't reach *him* and again I had let go of my wheel to get loose from *him*. When I started swinging on *him*, *he* locked my arms, so I bit *him*. When everything came to a stop, I turned my car back around and went home– where *he* stayed with me all day.

There was even a time we weren't speaking, and I ran into *him* at a party. I saw *him* talking to a bitch, so I walked up and swung on *him*. *He* ran after me in the party and ended up accidentally hitting my homegirl in the back of the head instead of me. I was so embarrassed because I knew niggas found out the truth that night.

I pulled up to *his* house the next morning to confront *him*, like nigga you really tried to sock me in my head in front of everybody? But *he* wasn't home, only his dad was. I couldn't even get the words out when trying to tell his dad without crying. When I told him his son tried to hit me he turned to me and said, "You don't think you guys could work it out?" I thought to myself, this nigga beats on his wife and just left in silence.

Days later, when I had the chance to talk to his mom about it, she asked me again, just to make sure that she heard me clear. "*He* hits you?". As if she were genuinely shocked, she looked at me with so much compassion and told me I needed to leave *him*. I loved her so much I felt like she was one of the main reasons I always stayed.

As a child, I watched my mom and dad cheat on each other. I saw my dad turn my mom the fuck out, ultimately breaking his own heart. While we hated exactly who our parents became, we became just like our parents.

Shortly after that, we went to a college basketball game together. At some point in the game, a football player who was also an old friend walked in. I didn't know at the time, but my boyfriend watched as he grabbed my attention. *He* just never mentioned it. After I seen him that day, we rekindle our friendship and I started confiding in him about what was going on in my relationship. I found myself crying in his bed one day, telling him I didn't want to be with my boyfriend anymore.

Days later my boyfriend came to my house. We were hanging out, and *he* snatched my phone then ran to my bathroom. *He* read a text that said, "I wish I could just be in your bed right now with you rubbing my head". When *he* came out of the bathroom to confront me, I had already ran out my house. I walked down a side street, only to I find him running after me. *He* grabbed me and coerced me to come back to my house so we could talk about it.

When I got close enough to my front door, I attempted to run inside so I could lock the door, but *he* grabbed and slammed me against the bench that sat on my front porch. *He* tried to talk to me, but all I could tell *him* was that I was sick. *He* told me *he* hated my parents for making me the way I was and if we broke up one more time, *he* was going to kill himself. So, I stayed.

But I couldn't take this shit. I couldn't live with my fucking self any longer and I wasn't going to live with *his* ass either. A week later, we met at a Cold Stones to talk and I ended things with *him*. As I stood up to leave, I kissed *his* forehead. I told *him* he was strong and that he could do it. I watched a tear roll down *his* face and realized I was really talking to myself. From the start, I loved *him* so much and for so long, but I was ready to start loving myself. I was drained from all the mental abuse. I was disgusted with the physical abuse. You would've thought I wanted to leave, but how could I leave what seemed to be the only person to love me unconditionally even after all the pain *he* caused? Only a baby when I met him, I was blinded by his love. I wouldn't be able to count how many times I attempted to give my life over *his* love.

AGONY

A week after that, I came to his house to "talk to *him*", but I really just wanted to get my belongings. Soon after we started talking, it got nowhere and I just wanted to leave, but *he* took my keys and wouldn't give them back. I was too scared to tell *him* I was really leaving, so I told *him* I needed a break and I promised I would come back. *He* told me if I wanted to leave, I'd have to suck *his* dick. When I said no, *he* replied "If you want to act like a hoe, Ima treat you like a hoe" then *he* told me again "If you want to leave you gonna suck my dick or we fucking".

All I wanted to do was leave because I couldn't take how toxic our relationship had become. I no longer wanted to be a part of it. I watched as *he* pulled out a condom to put on and I was confused because we never used them. I watched *him* rub his dick until it became fully lubricated, then *he* proceeded to take it off. I took my pants off and *he* told me to get on all four. A piece of me wanted to believe *he* thought *he* would save our relationship by making me have sex with *him,* but I just ended up getting raped by my own boyfriend.

Worth

Feelings of not being worthy
I'd stare in the mirror asking if I was worth it
Because I put all this work in
And still couldn't make this shit work man
All those times you hit me like I was worthless
It was you, the one I trusted, who made me forget my purpose
Called me all types of "hoes" when it was you who swore I
was perfect
From moaning "I love you" while fucking me gently
To bashing my head into my driver side window
Two different moments, both happened so quickly
It was you who showed me that I wasn't the only one who was
sick
Because how many times did you drag me out my car and
pretend like I asked for it
I felt you break my heart until you could no longer use it
"I'm in your life more than your parents are"
You were quick to mentally abuse it
Blaming me for your excuses

CRAZY PRAYER

Dear God,

Where is the thin line between reminiscing and dwelling in the past?

Can you tell me how I became trapped in this realm?

Can you show me where the thin line between being a realist and a pessimist is?

How did I become so blind to it?

Can you tell me how my unconditional love withered into pain, suffering, and resentment?

Am I that damaged, God?

Did I ask for any of this?

I'm not scared but confused.

Do I feel Lost?

No.

I feel Stolen.

When I think of how I was his best friend, mother, and lover for three years, I wonder...

Am I crazy?

I used to get my head smashed into my driver's window while trying to get us to our destination.

I remember the times I'd let go of the wheel to fight back.

Am I crazy?

Most people would say dumb,

not giving me the credit of having the courage at such a young age to love someone I gradually realized didn't even love their self.

I thought I could be the one to show him what unconditional love felt like.

What it looked like.

What it tasted like.

Am I crazy?

The moment I felt brave enough to say Enough is Enough

He told me he'd kill himself

so, I stayed.

Am I crazy?

DYAMOND IN THE ROUGH

I allowed myself to be mentally abused for 3 years.
I told him my secrets and my biggest fear.
Only for him to throw in my face at the lowest point in my life.
He confessed that he hated my parents for making me the way I
am
and told me I was going to be just like my mother.
Am I crazy?
When I finally decided I was leaving he called me heartless
yet the next week when I went to collect all my belongings
He.Raped.Me.
Am I crazy?
I laid there crying, with tears falling down my face on all four
With brown period blood smeared on my inner thighs
Hearing his laugh as he patronized me
"What?! You Feel Degraded?"
As he laughed again
No.
I was Defeated.
In that moment I just needed all of the pain he'd ever put me
through to be over
After 3 years I was ready for it to be over
Am I crazy?
I allowed myself to think that I Let Him rape me
Because I was too tired of fighting to fight back
Yet once he allowed me to grab my shit to leave
I had the audacity to grab my blade
And at the first red light that caught me
I dragged it through my arm
Over and over again
In attempts to dispel and cleanse what he ruined
Me.
And I Let Him
Am I crazy?
For having more than 100 cuts on my body that all symbolize
names–
Names of people Who Are Crazy

DYAMOND IN THE ROUGH

Dear Heavenly Mother,
I pray you never allow the pain in my trauma to defeat me or
to take away from my compassion and humanity
Broken, but I will not allow myself to fall victim to my
misfortunes
I will let go of all the agony so I can prove myself before I lose
myself

Dear God
Please forgive me for all the doubt I've fed myself
For all the hatred I've carried in my heart
For all the self- destruct
I Vow to Love Myself as I Evolve into Who I'm Destined to Be
ALADY

DYAMOND IN THE ROUGH

CHAPTER 4

Daddy's Little Girl, Dyamond

Dyme,

What is there to really say? I barely remember anything, and you know everything. I guess I'll start from the beginning. The first time I met you was at my house. I had invited some people over and you came with a blossoming social media star. I got drunk and wanted to throw him off the balcony. Before you left, we exchanged information, or maybe I hunted you down on Instagram.

Regardless, I later convinced you to come over for a swim. When you did, you brought a dejected sense of anger that radiated from you like a furnace. I found this to be very attractive because I was angry too. To this day I've never seen a body like that. Some thick little wannabe hood rat spilling all over the world. I felt lucky just to watch you jiggle. To watch you flop around in the water pretending to not give a fuck or know that I was watching you.

You wanted a drink, so we went inside. That's when I noticed the slashes all over your body. From wrist to elbow they zigzagged across butter soft skin. Skin so soft that even the smallest scar rose up like a great mountain. I had never seen anything like it. Hundreds of deep, long, thick slashes crammed under a tattoo that read **"Damon"**.

Who the fuck is Damon? What man could fuck a thousand scars onto a woman like you? Immediately jealous, insecure, and turned on. I wanted They to give you a scar. I wanted to cover your body in them. were on your thighs too, right next to your pussy. A bit more confidence and I would've pulled my dick out and stuck it in. You would've liked that. But I didn't.

Instead we talked and I felt weak and unworthy under your intensity. I remember trying to play it cool. But I couldn't resist the temptation to call you stupid. I told you that you act like you know and have been through everything, but you haven't. I told you that you didn't know shit. I meant it when I said it. But it wasn't true. **Soon I realized you love people that treat you like shit.**

Jimmy

2018

2014

I'm that Girl
scarred by her father's insecurities
my daddy lost his mind
and I lack purity

I fall for the same niggaz-
who act like the same nigga-
my momma got tatted on her titty

my daddy does drugs
and I fuck niggaz
who wouldn't even know I'm this witty

my daddy does drugs
and stopped giving a fuck about me clearly

Never Trust tatted on my face
plotting on the wrong niggaz
to take Daddy's place

2014

Scorpio Girl

Why is your mind always in the wrong place?

How do so many people love you
Yet you're filled with so much hate

You fell victim to lust and now you're lost
And don't even know your place

Walking around confused because your period is late
You thought you could trust that one nigga, but you got played

Vulnerable
I guess you got a few of your mother's traits

They say the apple doesn't fall far from the tree

And at the same time, you just like your daddy
Always faded
Alcohol Dependency

How will you ever be free
If you keep drowning yourself in your dead lover's sea

Do you know what it feels like to have to search for the man
who never in his life should have lost you
I gave you an ultimatum and you chose it over me
How could you leave yet swear you love me?
You broke my mother's heart and now that you played me
You're hiding
You knew I'd be home in December and you were nowhere to
be found
So here I am feeling like
I Am Nothing
But I Am Your Reflection
You hurt me to the core
So now I move in deception
You hide from me because of what you're ashamed of
You chose crack over your 11-year-old daughter
That's something you should fucking be ashamed of
You think you've escaped your demons
But really your demons lay here and taunt me
You abandoned me when I was 11
And at 12 I lost my virginity
I compared myself to all the other 12-year-old girls who had
dads
And wondered where mine was at?
Yeah, I pushed you away because I thought my love was
More Than Crack
2013

Daddy >

Text Message
Today 7:56 PM

(1/2) Tho
i may have the most selfish way of
showing it
knowin who da most
blessed iz
there
nutting i can say or write to let you
nowut u deserve
blindness

(2/2) continues
defeating me

i wish i could be there

DYAMOND IN THE ROUGH

December 2013

Dear Father,

I heard you had another seizure and when Papa Andre found you, you had blood oozing out your mouth. If he didn't notice Ditto's barking, who knows if you would still be alive. I'd like to think I wish I'd been there, but then I can't help but to flash back to your very first seizure. I was only 9 years old, we were at the apartment in Leimert Park and I watched the whole thing. From you playing with me, to you falling out, and me thinking you were still playing. I then heard the strange noises you were making from struggling and stared in complete fear at your eyes were rolling to the back of your head. It took 3 adults to get my 9-year-old body out the living room. I was screaming at the top of my lungs as they locked me in the kitchen. I can still hear vividly, Papa Andre yelling "Grab his tongue".

Fast forward to January 2012, the day of Aunt Nikki's funeral. As we all got ready to send her off, I heard Aunt CT whisper "Watch Damon". As I watched this time, I was 17 years old. It happened just as quickly as the first time. You spaced out and before you could fall, Uncle George caught you and grabbed your tongue. No different from when I was 9 years old, my 17-year-old body went into shock and I was screaming. The same exact emotions rushed my brain. Terrified from the thought of losing the only man I've ever loved unconditionally; my entire existence. I cursed Aunt CT out so bad for buying you the alcohol the previous days before. I couldn't even believe you did that shit on the day of your sister's funeral. A day where Taylor, Josh, and I needed you. We all needed each other.

After you were discharged from the hospital, Uncle Joey sent you back to LA and a year later when I graduated, I moved back home too. Months later, you have this seizure, where Papa Andre found you and it got back to me. And I sit here and wonder — Would I have wiped the blood from your mouth? Would I have had the strength to hold your tongue? Or would I have been screaming from the top of my lungs for help?

A hopeless 19-year-old daddy's girl. I found myself searching for you for two weeks and then I got a phone call from

65

Papa Andre. He told me "your girlfriend" called and said you were incarcerated. Fuck that Bitch for being the first to know. You called her first? I don't even know this woman and I have to hear about you from her.

After that feeling, I would always search your name online and sometimes, just a piece of me, just a piece of my heart, would just pray to God that they kept you in that cell. I've always known you had demons. Aunt Nikki told me about the abandonment issues you endured with your parents. I watched you and my mother break each other hearts to a point of no return and because of that I feel all the pain you both caused each other.

Remember in 2010, when I came home to LA. You were my very last stop. A very awkward, and distant visit. At the end, I asked CT if she had a pen and paper. When she handed them to me, I wrote a note and slipped it to you. As we buckled our seat beats, you ran out of the apartment and up to the car to give me a kiss and to tell me you love me.

The note said. "DON'T BE ASHAMED, WE ALL HAVE OUR OWN ADDICTIONS". A year later in 2011, Aunt Nikki moved you to Texas, and that's when you saw my scarred body. I could see in your eyes, that you understood exactly what my note meant.

Dad, do you remember when you found me blacked out in my room one night? I don't. I can't even imagine what I looked like when you walked in. I only remember waking up and noticing my blade missing. I ran into your room and demanded you give me my blade back. All those fresh cuts you saw on my wrist and my neck. You told me it was your fault. You took my blade and kept my secret. So, I refused to not judge you because you never judged me.

People keep insisting that if I keep fighting your battles, I will continue to suffer in so much pain. But I don't give a fuck. I'm tired of my friends seeing you on the street belligerently drunk out your mind. I'm tired of having to spy and search for my own father. Witnessing you beg for change in front of liquor stores. And I'm fed up that when I finally find you, you've been beaten on and bruised up. I just want my daddy back. -**Love Dyme Ski**

Nov 7th, 2015, 10:22 AM

Hi daddy!
I want you to know I think
you're amazing.
Flaws and all
And you made me a strong
woman,
Teaching me unconditional love

Well I got a lot of making up to
do it's never 2 late starting with
you and Oooooohhhh
Weeeeee! And den da
Grandbayyybayyy ;)))))
Luv U

Nov 10, 2015, 4:35 PM

You going to be mama and I'm
going 2 be a grandpapé (:0{
Yeeeeeeeeeaaaaaahhhhhh

67

DYAMOND IN THE ROUGH

2018

Holding in every emotion you ever passed down to me, my
peers call me mean.
Even you have called me mean.
You've gone so far to tell me "Fuck You" and even called me
an "Asshole"
Yet it was you, who passed down to me, this angry bitterness.
All from keeping in my pain and suffering in attempt to make
everybody around me who I care about enough content with life.

Today is April 3rd and it's one of my best friend's birthday but
guess what? I don't feel like celebrating it with her. And guess
why? Because I just found out you got booked with a felony on
April 1st... My other best friend's birthday...
April's Fool... you are a fool.
And I am a bigger fool for not being able to control my fucking
emotions because of you...

I am 23 years old and intelligent.
Known as a free spirit but here's my truth:
I am caged in, trapped;
Dwelling in the misery of all the issues
you have passed down to me as a child and teenage adult
that are all from your own unresolved childhood issues.

I am 23 years old with a beautiful, perfect, almost 2-year-old
daughter.
Who is climbing all over my fragile body, as I sit here writing
this, with what seems to be infinite tears falling from my eyes.
Bitch.

How am I supposed to play with my daughter with tears–
tears that feel endless coming out my eyes?
Tears that burn more than all your broken promises that have
ever set my soul on fire.
In. The. Worst. Way.
Bitch.

DYAMOND IN THE ROUGH

If I ever killed myself, I pray you know it was all because of
you.
My whole life I believed in you.
Little did I know you never even believed in yourself.
For 21 years you had me fooled.
I had me fooled.
Because not until the most important day of my life did you
show me...
You.

I found you in Leimart Park when I was four months pregnant
but I wanted to wait until a sober day came to tell you.
In the midst of waiting, you asked me to take you to your court
hearing the following week,
and I did.

It was your first day sober...
But it didn't go as you planned,
I noticed when you signed in, that your hand was shaking
then moments went by quickly to where I watched you zone
out.
I caught you.
4 months pregnant and all.
Terrified, screaming at the police.
You didn't even allow the EMT to take you to the hospital, so I
had to take you home.
Where you end up having multiple seizures and had no choice,
but to go to the hospital.

I came and visited you in the hospital.
I knew you'd be sober for a couple days after and that's when I
handed you my ultrasound.
I told you I needed you.
I told you my daughter needed her grandfather because she
didn't have a father.
Two days later, you were sober.

DYAMOND IN THE ROUGH

Fast Forward 6 Months Later:
On the most important day of my life did you open my eyes to
how oblivious I've always been.
On my due date You went missing.
You Fucking Went Missing Dude.
We spent my whole pregnancy together.
Eating whatever we wanted, bonding as the best friends
I've always knew we were.
More importantly: WE WERE SOBER TOGETHER.

You waited until April 10th, to relapse.
You. Selfish. Weak. Ass. Nigga.
But Marz didn't come that day...
And I spent it crying in my bed... ALONE.
Until you had the audacity to show up to my house, reeking of
cheap ass vodka.
And when you walked in my room
I cried out "WHAT THE FUCK BRO?"
with tears pouring out my eyes.
And all you could say was
"Dyamond, I'm scared"
and I got even more angry and screamed
"BITCH THIS ISN'T YOUR BABY".

I got induced on April 17th, 2016,
And for 6 months I envisioned You, my Father, my best friend,
cutting my daughter's umbilical cord.
But I was foolish–
Foolish to believe in you, when you never even fucking
believed in yourself.
You called to say you were on your way
but I could hear how drunk you were.
I told you if you came, I would call the police on you.
But even then,
I hoped you'd show up...
Still.
At least sat in the lobby until you became sober...

70

DYAMOND IN THE ROUGH

After 6 long hours of anticipation, I felt my first contraction
and you still weren't there.
There was only 3 people in that room when I got my epidural.
The anesthesiologist, the nurse and me.
ALONE.
I had heard all about how big the needle was,
yet I was so angry at you.
I knew when they told me to take a deep breath,
to think of You.
I knew to think of all the emotional pain, you had ever caused
me because

On the most important day of my life,
You weren't there.
How am I supposed to play with my daughter with tears— tears
that feel endless coming out my eyes?

You see in my last therapy session,
I told my therapist that I wanted to write a book on my
childhood.
But she told me she didn't want me to talk about everything I
been through by myself.
I thought she was just brushing me off, but after writing this
letter to you...
I see that she was only trying to protect me.
From Me.

Because writing this and having to relive it...
Dad,
Nah fuck that.
Damon,
If I ever killed myself, I pray you know it was all because of
you.
But if I ever committed suicide,
that would make me just like you,
A deadbeat.

So, Reflect and Tell Me This:
How am I supposed to play with my daughter with tears—tears that have always felt never ending coming out my eyes?

DYAMOND IN THE ROUGH

Damon Taylor
BKG# 5272224
Terminal Annex
PO. BOX 86164
Los Angeles, CA 90086

Hello My Dyme Ski and Marzee Pooh,
I am so sorry for the way I've been so cruel. I am very spoiled and dumb. I have two of the most beautiful babies a dad could ever dream of and here I am neglecting my reality. I love you so much Dyamond, my eyeglasses are getting foggy. I really have a horrible way of showing it, well... no excuses. I just wasn't brought up in your "American family" way. I pray for you and Marzee Pooh all of the time, even before I was in this situation. That's kind of the way I kept my sanity from not talking to you or anybody else I wish was still here with me. It is a real deep problem that I've dealt with since I was 9 years old when I felt abandoned, and still feel the same way to this day. Please forgive me for expressing this to you. It is my first time even telling anybody this. I love you Dyamond. I would do anything for you if I'm capable. Anything. PLEASE PLEASE PLEASE I BEG YOU TO ACCEPT MY APOLOGY.
Your Dad and Grandpa,
Damon Taylor (Smile)

HAPPY MOTHER'S DAY DYME SKI.
See ya soon. May 10th, 2018

LOVEU2DEATH

Laying in my sanctuary of water that's hot
Contemplating whether he loves me or not
Baptizing myself in my own sacred thoughts

Reflecting on the thin lines my body shows of love and hate
Stuck in between my dreams and waking up to fate

He told me to come see him at the crossroads
The first time we ever crossed roads

As I got to the gate, I watched true colors showed
I stood there bodiless as my destiny unfold

Something about me "sinning"
My savior went missing when I stopped forgiving
My wrist was dripping from my blade slipping
I had battled myself for so long to see if my love was really
worth risking

Drowned in my bathtub of an ocean
While my soul lingered on Earth floating
because
it wasn't my time to go.

74

DYAMOND IN THE ROUGH

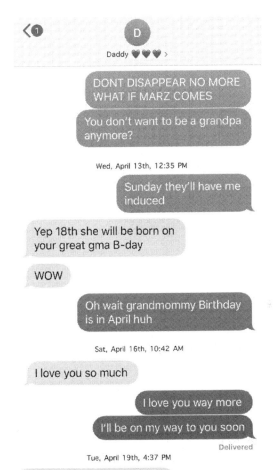

DYAMOND IN THE ROUGH

Denies SI. "i don't allow myself to".

"i wouldn't want to do anything to jeopardize her (dau) being put in the system".

Not cut on self for 1 1/2yrs.

Short Term Goals:
Reduce depression and anger

Meet *Frank Andre Taylor Jr.*

Thursday, March 5th, 2015
2:33 pm

Fka: Dre Taylor
Bka: Papa Andre

Born: December 5th, 1948
Sun: Sagittarius Moon: Aquarius

Occupation: Former Pimp

Favorite Singers: James Brown
Major Love/ Soulmate: Candice aka Candy aka Grandma Candy

Have you ever apologized to my father for abandoning him?
Papa Andre: Abandon? Well, his mother went to the penitentiary. His mother loved him Dyamond, but whatever happened— she didn't have a choice. The kid never understood that. The only reason he was with me in Hawaii—I never wanted my son to be around that element. I never wanted my son to get in the life.

You didn't want him to get in the life?
Papa Andre: Aww, hell no. Because what I was doing… I had women and stuff like that. You know what I'm saying? I just didn't want him to be that. He was playing basketball, in school doing good. But he felt as though, his mother…like [a woman] — you don't know Dyamond. She's cried so many times. She just didn't have a choice. She did 6 years in the penitentiary. I didn't abandon my son, I made an agreement with my mom rather than keeping him with me in that bad element.

I can see what you're saying but—
Papa Andre: Did it have an effect?

It's still kind of abandon— Like maybe [you] think you didn't abandon him. But as a child he definitely felt abandoned.
Papa Andre: Oh! But guess what? You're right. So does he have issues? There were some negative effects as a parent. I loved my son. We were doing cool. I was still dealing with the situation, so that's why mom had to take care of Damon.

Yeah, that makes sense but that's exactly how I felt when I had to live with my grandma. The feeling of abandonment clearly stuck with my father, because he abandoned me— only to make me feel how you made him feel.

Did my dad know his mother went to the penitentiary or did you lie to him?
Papa Andre: Yeah, he knew, we were honest. Maybe we should've lied because I was in the life. He was only in grade school. The police wanted me, and she loved me so much that she wouldn't sign off on any papers. The girl was good, the police told her if she signed the paperwork on me that she could've walked. She was dedicated and that's why I love her until this day. She went to prison for me. Maybe I did make the mistake of telling Damon the truth, because here he had a dad and lost his mom and he was hurt. He grew angry at her, but it wasn't her fault. But he was a boy and he needed his mother. If he would've had his mother, things would've probably been different. I didn't realize the damage it would do to him. I was young and crazy.

So, if you could've gone to prison instead of her, would you have?
Papa Andre: Hell No. It was better her than me. I'm a survivor.

I'm saying for my dad's sake
Papa Andre: I had hundreds of thousands of dollars. I just think it would've been a lot easier for a white woman, than a black man in prison. He had diamonds and gold growing up. He didn't know how many people were jealous of him. He was spoiled. I know it was rough on him, I didn't mean for that to happen.

So, did my dad ever see his mom after she got released from prison?

Papa Andre: Oh yeah! He went to see her when she got out in Hawaii… But she couldn't be with me. She was on parole and I just wasn't going to do that to her. See Candy messed up because she never wrote Damon, and after a while of her being in there she started to resent me. When she got out, she had to get back on her feet. She started being around these rich Arabian men.

I didn't want to deprive my son from his mother, but I wasn't going to have him around no white man. And she didn't have no choice when it came to Damon. She made the best choice when it came to Damon. She could not have another man around my son that loved her but was going to be jealous of my son who was half white and half black. He was just best being with my mom. My mother was a hard worker, and she was stern. What I was doing was against our religion. I didn't grow up to be like this, I was angry at the white man though! And I had rather him be with someone I loved [my mother], than all the women I was around.

So, I guess the answer was No.

Let's Play a Game

My dad was in my life consistently up until I turned 9 years old. He just stopped coming around, but that didn't stop my love for him. I'd write his name all over my notebooks. "Lil Damon" "Daddy's Girl" "Lil Ski Mask", to the point where my mom would say "If you love him so much go live with him". But I didn't have the slightest idea of where my father even lived (if I did, like duh I would go move with him— tf).

When I was 13 years old, I was on my way to World On Wheels with my best friend Ashley. As we were driving up Crenshaw, passing up 48th, I seen a homeless man with a bag over his shoulders full of cans. I wasn't sure of who I saw, but at 13 years old my soul told me to hop out that car. I didn't even care that we were in the middle of traffic. I asked my best friend's cousin to stop his car. He was so confused. I then proceeded to hop out of his moving car and start running. I ran down half the block... until I was behind who I thought I saw. "DADDY?" I said, my voice was shaking... He slowly turned around and replied back, "I look terrible huh?". My raggedy ass gone shake my head, yes.

In 2016, 8 days before my daughter was born he did the absolute UNTHINKABLE and abandoned me because he was "scared". For those of you who don't know, my father is an alcoholic addict (like me... maybe I'm like him). Anyway, my dad was incarcerated on March 31st, 2018. Since then, I've had time (not enough) to forgive him and restart my healing process. Especially with knowing he's off the street.

I told my stepmom and Papa Andre that I wouldn't talk to him unless they told him that I wanted a letter from him apologizing. He wrote it and I received it (in every way). From age 15 to hell 24, ain't no telling how many times me and my father have had to get to know each other over and over again. No matter how awkward it was, no matter how impatient and angered I was... I was always down for the cause and he's always been the most understanding, even when I didn't want to understand him.

Except this time, as his 24-year-old adult child with no uppity tone or sarcasm and hardly any resentment left in my heart. I wrote to him "Let's play a game. You tell me a story about your mom and I'll tell you a story about mine. You tell me a story about your dad and I'll tell you one about my dad".

Y'all see what I did there? I had to trick this nigga to open up to me, but damn that shit really worked my nigga... The next letter I got in the mail he told me about his mom, which he's never done before.

On February 15th, my dad wrote me a letter that enclosed this

"So I'm going to try your writing game. Don't judge my writing, the sloppier it gets the more of the truth I'm telling.

Introduction: What's the deal 6/11 in the da 1970's, here comes... wait not yet! My mom's not ready for me. False Alarm. My Dad says "Nah B*tch! You having this baby" and gave her some kind of castor oil so I could get into this cold world and she could "make his money". Tonight, is like Supa Fly. The Real Super Fly (the more classic Super Fly). But GOD did not like my dad's actions and had a skunk spray him for rushing his progress. On God! My mom was so pissed she named me Damon Anthony Powell... whut the hell? My mom's name was Virginia Powell. Now it's Candy which my dad changed along with mine to Damon Andre Taylor.

I can remember my mom from the time I was able to see a white woman naked bathing me, the FACES just changed til I was 7. That's when apparently my Real mom just got out the pen for robbery (it's in my blood, wow) in Hawaii. I finally saw her when I turned 9 and met her at 26.

So Dyamond, I've seen my mom one more time than you have. *smiley face* Gemini *sad face* (switch) just like my personality"

And he went on to change the subject...

My father has silenced his emotional pain all his life and suppressed his abandonment issues. Almost like his disregarded them in a way. Over time, his poor decisions showed how effected and hurt he truly was. By him opening up to me and telling me that he's only met his mother one more time than me, that shit hurt my feelings... and shit— my daddy is more sensitive than me so I can only imagine how he has felt his whole life.

However, don't let your mommy issues turn into your daughter having daddy issues.

SELF-HATE:
A Read for Papa Andre

For a long time, I didn't see anything wrong with my Papa Andre pimping white women as a means to retaliate against the white man from years of trauma and oppression. As I began reflecting on the outcome of what happened as a result of him laying down with those same women and making babies he didn't even want, I now see how my father became the product of his own environment.

June 1, 2019
12:30 pm

I'm working on forgiving Grandpa Frank for causing so much dysfunction in our family.
Papa Andre: Well... you don't know my father and I'm not dysfunctional.

Way to add insult to injury with your son who just got out of jail at 3 am in the backseat and your emotionally challenged granddaughter in the front.
Papa Andre: My son ain't perfect and neither was I.

You thought you were superior to the white man by pimpin his women when that made you no better. You didn't even honor yourself as a black man to have been able to uplift and honor a black woman in your lifetime. You laid down with these white women and made babies, one growing up motherless and the other, fatherless.
Papa Andre: Well the one who grew up fatherless, that was out of my control— they just up and left. My other son is handsome and I bet the people at KRST (the spiritual center I go to) look at you and get jealous.

No, they probably look at me weird because of the colorist ideologies that you have tried to instill in me growing up in regard to skin color and privilege. However, your handsome son is on drugs. Thank God Uncle Brandon got away because he seems to be doing just fine without you being around as his dad.

Papa Andre: That's okay, but what about your other grandma? She's a white woman and she married a black man who was a damn cop...

And she still acknowledged he was a King and treated him as such. You think I'm really worried about your white hoes, when the woman of my world who raised and tried to protect me most of my life is white. I have a lot of forgiving to do with my ancestors not just Grandpa Frank.

Papa Andre: You don't know my father and what he went through.

Okay, I understand the trauma of it all, but how long are you gonna keep blaming your faults on the white man instead of taking accountability for what you as a black man have put your family through? You're right, I didn't know Grandpa Frank. What I do know is that he did not honor my great Grandma Claudia in the laws of marriage.

Papa Andre: Well I hope your marriage turns out fine.

First of all, I told that nigga to pull over and let me out his car. I don't know why he thought I needed his backwards ass blessing. Second of all, what in the self-hate has this nigga instilled in his own son? What is handsome in equivalence to being broken? Third of all, I almost gagged at him telling me the black women at my spiritual center were probably jealous of the way I look. I know my Grandma Claudia has to be turning over in her grave from this egotistical ass misogynist. Lastly, how can a man defend his father on adultery against his own mother instead of acknowledging his mistake? Instead, he attempts to justify it by saying "You don't know what my father went through". What I do know in my heart is that this man's decision to step out on his family and create another one caused a lot of dysfunction and division between our family as a whole.

Patient Name: Dyamond L Taylor
MRN: ▓▓▓▓▓▓▓
DOB: 11/3/1994 Sex: F
Date of Visit: 12/2/2016

DYAMOND IN THE ROUGH MEDICAL OFFICE

Lots of stress and anger and sadness related to father's alcohol addition and inability to maintain sobriety and be a consistent father figure in her life.

Family History:
Mother - patient's mother has history of depression
Father - patient reports that her father is an "alcoholic" and has history of depression

CHAPTER 5

For Children Trapped in the Dyamond Mine

DYAMOND IN THE ROUGH MEDICAL OFFICE

Taylor, Dyamond L
MRN: ▓▓▓▓▓▓
DOB: 11/3/1994, Sex: F

Date of Visit:
6/28/2017

TPI RESULTS REVIEWED: YES

CRITICAL ALERTS PRESENT:YES

CRITICAL ALERTS ADDRESSED: YES

PHQ-9: 15 GAD-7: 17

Chief Complaint: Medication Management

Subjective: Dyamond L Taylor is a 22 year old female, with Major Depressive Disorder and Unhealthy Alcohol Use and Unhealthy Substance Use. She reports that she continues to feel depressed and "irritated". Reports that she is preoccupied with thoughts about past abuse, especially related to feels that her mother neglected her. She is currently living with her mother. She reports that she feels frustrated to be living with her. Patient reports that she continues to have disturbed sleep due to lack of trust, reports "I'm tossing and turning the whole night".

HYDE PARK AND BEACH

We woke up early one Sunday morning to go to brunch with my mother and her trick. Before we left the house, Brandee asked me for a hoodie. After we were sat down and told the waiter what we wanted, my mom spotted hickies on Brandee's neck. She looked at her with the sickest side eye and said, "Mmm-mm BJ, who gave you them monkey bites?". I immediately said, "ME" because I didn't want Brandee to get in trouble. My mom then countered my reply with the most off the wall look.

When we got home, Brandee confessed to my mom that the hickies were from the chick who lived above us. Later that night, my mom left and didn't come back. We decided not to go to school. To our surprise, my mom showed up to the house at 10 in the morning yelling and mad that we were "ditching". In reality, we just didn't feel like walking 45 minutes to school and when she stopped coming home, I stopped going.

She told us to get up and get ready for school. We got in the car and rode to school in complete silence. We could tell she was mad and before I got out the car, she demanded that I gave her my sidekick. So, I did give it to her— turned off.

Fast forward to after school, Brandee, Mel, and I got into the car. My mom turned to Brandee and said, "You going home". We all knew I was in trouble and by the time we got to Beach and La Brea, my mom asked for the password to my phone. I told her "NO". Plain and simple— NO! I guess she was so baffled that she asked me what I said. Again, I told her "N O". She then proceeded to pull the car over and I turned to Mel and said, "If she touches me, call the police". He said, ok.

She opened my door, climbed on me, and started socking me in my head repeatedly. I began choking her and told her "Get yo fat ass off me!". When I got a look at Mel, I could see the paralyzing fear in his eyes. All I could think was "This nigga really not calling the police". When I checked back into my reality, I could hear my mom screaming "So you gonna hit your mom?"

When she finally got off of me, she got out the back seat to return to her's. As she turned around, she must've seen all these firefighters who happened to be outside and screamed, "CALL THE POLICE I

DON'T GIVE A FUCK!". She then proceeded to drive off. We were only 5 mins away— if that, from our apartment on Hyde Park and Beach. When we pulled back into the parking lot and got out the car she said, "If you wanna call the police, call them" and I replied, "How, if you got my phone???". She handed me her phone nonchalantly. When I started dialing, I called my grandpa first and told him I was calling the police on my mom. After he asked me "HUH?" for the 4th time, I hung up on him and called 911. I called twice— for them not to even pick up…

When my mom walked into the house, she told me to strip naked and go get a belt. I was 13 years old and I told her no. I refused to get naked just so she could continue to beat me. She began punching me vigorously. All I kept hearing was this voice in my head saying, "Don't hit her, you love her". With each blow, I screamed for what seemed to be my life while Mel was outside bringing a box in from the car for my mom. In between the repeated punches to my head, I heard glass being shattered. It was Mel dropping the box to run into our apartment. By that point, I wasn't quite conscious. I could faintly hear him ask my mom, "Why are you doing this to her? We love you".

When I gained my consciousness back, I got up and ran into the bathroom to looked into the mirror. I was greeted by my left temple immensely swollen and bulging out my head. I could barely see straight. I was terrified. My vision was going in and out. My mother asked me one more time for my password and I told her "4120". As she went to her room to grab my phone, I turned to Mel and said, "I'm running away". He said okay, but he clearly had failed to register what I had said because when I got to the front door he yelled, "WAIT WHAT?". By the time he could fully comprehend what was going on, I had already started running.

I was halfway down my block screaming and crying trying to put my hair up in a bun. As I ran my fingers through my hair, it all started coming out in clumps. With each strand that fell, I started to relive what had happened to me. She… my mother, had her fingers gripped so tight in my full head of hair as she swung my head into the walls of that apartment that I lost consciousness. Much of my hair had fell out during the process.

I finally found a woman standing outside and asked her if I could use her phone— *Jamaican Woman around the corner.* She brought me inside her house and asked me what happen to me. When I told her my mother beat me, she asked, "Why…". She had the nerve to ask me "why" as if it fucking mattered. Then she said, "You can use my phone as long as you don't call the police on your mother because I have kids and I wouldn't want them to call the police on me". I agreed and she stared me down to make sure I didn't dial those 3 numbers.

I couldn't remember anybody's number, so I called Mel's mom Sandi. Sandi came shortly after and questioned me as well.

"Why wouldn't you give her the password"

"—She didn't buy the phone, nor does she put minutes on it. It's my privacy"

"What are you hiding on it?"

"Nothing…"

"What about you lying for Brandee? You shouldn't have done that…"

"I didn't want her to get in trouble"

"So, you rather get in trouble for her?"

We got in her car and she took me back home. I'd never been more devastated. At that moment, I felt like there was no escaping this life I was living. I got back to my house to find my Uncle Magic there. When I walked through the door my mother was standing in the kitchen, getting herself hyped— acting as if she was going to run up and attack me again. Sandi took her outside to calmed her down. As I was sitting right next to the front door in tears, my Uncle Magic walked over to me and whispered, "You want me to take out your sim card and put mine in?" *GOOD OLD UNCLE MAGIC.* I nodded my head yes. Moments later, my mom came back in the house and said "Magic, go get her phone". He went in her room and grabbed it, then came out and gave it to her. When the coast was clear, Uncle Magic walked past me and smoothly handed me my sim card which I hid in the inside of my cheek in my mouth.

Now it was my mom, Sandi, Uncle Magic, and Mel in the living room. When she asked me for my code one last final time I gave it to her. She got in with no problem— only it was empty. Everybody sat there confused, but my mother was filled with rage. She asked me why nothing was on it then Sandi's turned to me and asked, "If nothing was on there, why wouldn't you give her the password?" I told them it was the principle of privacy. She never bought me a phone nor anything that was needed for my phone, so what did she need my password for?

They were all salty, but the night didn't end there. The doorbell rang and to my surprise it was my Auntie BJ with Brandee. Brandee looked so sad when she walked in— as if she'd already known what was coming. When she saw my face, I could see all the sadness in her eyes morph into anger. She immediately began crying while holding my face saying "This ain't right".

Dyamond in the Rough Guidance Center
Dyamond Taylor
DOB: 11/3/94
Sex: F

Date: 2011

PROGRESS NOTE   Session #: 6

Description of session, including behavioral obeservations and response to treatment:

Pt said she did not enjoy her time in CA last week. Pt talked about her bio Mo being "Stupid and annoying". She said that she does not like her Mo but does not "hate" her. Pt did reveal some things of her childhood getting into a physical altercation with her bio Mo when pt was 13y/o and Mo telling her things that were verbally abusive about her not being pretty or Mo making faces when pt felt she looked good. Pt said she does hope to have less of a relationship with family members when she is an adult. She was also open about depressive thoughts. She said she has not had self-harm thoughts, just expressed feeling "sad" that she does not have anyone close to her. She also said that while in CA it felt like her grandmother who raised her was also turning against her.

Assessment of progress in treatment and current functioning:
Pt was less depressed today and able to continue working on relationship dynamics with family

Not in Your *Care*

I visited LA one summer per usual and you stopped by Aunt Rita's house to come see me. As I distanced myself from you, I found myself sitting on the edge of the pool, while everybody else swam. I was 16 years old and had been living in Texas for 2 years at this point. I ignored any call you ever tried to make and any text messages you ever sent. I could not stand you, but I was being forced to be in your presence. During this particular visit, I was cordial for Aunt Nikki's sake. You swam over to me for small talk, you know, attempted to catch up with me. While you noticed nobody wasn't paying attention, you grabbed my arm that had fresh scars on it, and then told me that I never did that to myself when I was in your care.

Audacity: *boldness or daring, especially with confident or arrogant disregard for personal safety, conventional thought, or other restrictions.*

Fast forward to when I was 21 years old, when I attempted to almost tell you my secret or at least I was willing to, just to be able to find out some of your truth. Curious as to how exactly you ended up so fucked up, I asked you if you'd ever been molested. You said *no* then asked me if I'd ever been. As much as I wanted to tell you the whole truth, I could only get out the word yes, before you'd interrupt me by saying "No you didn't. Well, not in my care". Infected from the deep denial you've always lived in; your words have always been a slap in my fucking face.

Not in your care?

You: *as a silly or stupid person; a person who lacks judgment or sense.* **A *fool*.** It took me many years to figure out that you weren't stupid at all. Silly, yes but stupid? No.

Everybody has always been merciful towards you and the decisions you've made your whole life. Making excuses for you, while some begged me to stall you out because you're *sick and not all there*. You've had the whole family convinced but I learned you.

DYAMOND IN THE ROUGH

Manipulative: *influencing or attempting to influence the behavior or emotions of others for one's own purposes.*

And you must be *smart* to be able to manipulate.

LA BREA AND WESTHAVEN

Dreading certain flashbacks that my memory won't erase, every time I must drive down La Brea, I am reminded of how much my parents put me off with a family member.

In this case, specifically my greats- aunts. My dad stayed in the front room and my aunts' bedroom was in the back. My dad would always be there when I got dropped off. We'd bond over an episode of COPS, as I laid down to go to bed– then he'd go run the streets with his friends.

Leaving me unsettled and paranoid because my imagination would incite my deepest fears. I'd psych myself into thinking something bad would happen to my dad and I'd never see him again. I'd think of every "what if" I could come up with like, how easy it would be for a serial-murderer-rapist to break in and kill me. Plus, the loud ass traffic on La Brea Ave didn't help put my nerves to ease neither. So, when he was ready to leave, he'd ignore my crying and begging, then put me in my Aunts' room.

The first time I ever hurt myself was at the white house on the corner of La Brea and Westhaven Street, after being told that my dad wasn't coming back so I had better stop crying. I did. I stopped crying right after I dragged a wire hanger through my 9-year-old arm, not even understanding what I just did to myself.

20 Years Old

I was in the kitchen putting up the food I had just bought when you walked in. You examined the two jars of pickles and pack of 7-Up I had in my arms and then said "OOH, YOU PREGNANT". At this point I didn't really care to say yes or no, I was so annoyed I said, "So What". I didn't hear much from you after that because I barely even spoke to you.

I never decided when exactly I was going to tell grandma but of course, I wanted it to be special. It never came to my mind that you would have told her, even after her asking me so many times when my period was coming. It was weird, however, that she kept asking because she had never in my life ever been concerned about my period.

When she finally told me she knew, she told me you told her. Which I wondered why? It was none of your business to even tell. Why would you ruin a moment like that for me? She later sat me down and began to sob, telling me you told her it was her fault that I got pregnant.

You told an 88-year-old woman that it was her fault that my 20-year-old ass got pregnant. What in the manipulation was going on in your mind? How did that even make sense to you coming out your mouth? Because she allowed my 20-year-old self to have guest spend the night?

But the gag was, my baby's father had never been to our house. He didn't even know where I stayed so not only did you ruin a special moment for me and my grandma, but then you tried to guilt trip and manipulate her into thinking my pregnancy was not only a mistake but her fault.

I was **20 years old**, not 16 *SUS*.

DYAMOND IN THE ROUGH

Part 2

The first time I felt my daughter kick, I was too geeked. I jumped up and begged my friend Gil to put his hand on my stomach, but he was a little freaked out and I understood. The emotions I felt though, the happiness I felt. I was so excited that when I sat up, my brand-new headboard hit the wall.

I hadn't even noticed that my headboard had hit the wall, until I started to hear you talk real crazy and loud. I got out my bed to see what was wrong with you and when I walked into the living room, you said something to the effect of "You not gonna be fucking in my grandma's house."

I was so confused yet, my whole body filled with anger. Before you could say anything else, I said, "Shut Up Bitch" and walked back in my room. How dare you… 1) Accuse me of something so inappropriate

and disrespectful at such a happy moment like this. 2) Be so concerned about my 20 years old pussy that belonged to me.

You followed me to my room screaming "OH IM A BITCH, YOU A HOE. YOU FUCKING A NIGGA WHILE YOU PREGNANT WITH ANOTHER NIGGA'S BABY".

I just sat there in disbelief that you'd even say anything like that, in front of the person. I was disgusted and embarrassed because me and him weren't being anywhere near sexual.

I just shared this special moment of feeling my baby's first kick with my friend and you came up with some sick ass shit in your own mind and decided to run off it.

When he came to talk to you to try and calm you down, you told him "You think you the only one? You not", in which he responded, "That's fine, because we weren't having sex".

Who the fuck says that? Who the fuck says that about their own daughter to their daughter's friend? You told the both of us that you had something coming for us. Grandma told us to ignore you and to get some sleep. I cried myself to sleep that night while he held me and my baby.

DYAMOND IN THE ROUGH

Dear Toy,

After today everything should be clear. All you do is hurt me and it's been evident since birth that you are unhealthy for me. You've allowed your demons to consume you; therefore, I used it as an excuse to always forgive you. Today, I've come to the conclusion that your actions have no logic. I refuse to continue to sweep all the pain, hurt, and bullshit you've put me though underneath your rug. I believe that our relationship is broken beyond repair and I wish to discontinue all forms of communications with you for the safety of me and my daughter. The fucked-up part is that I've always been willing to forgive you, yet you've never failed to surprise me with your disrespectful actions. Yesterday you reminded me about all the pain and trauma you've ever caused, specifically during my childhood. If I were still that weak little girl, I would've cut into my skin to not feel everything you did. But the love I have for my daughter, already, will always be stronger than the love you've ever shown me my entire life. I would like you to realize that you'll never love anybody until you find love and comfort within yourself. Hopefully, one day, you'll have enough courage to conquer your demons and stop letting them eat you alive. Until then, don't shoot me a text asking how I'm doing or lying about how much you love and miss me. Don't attempt to pretend you're trying to help me, don't try and hug me, and most importantly stay away from my belly. I don't need your tainted soul tarnishing me or my daughter's golden aura (or soul if you can't understand).

Sincerely and forever genuine,
Dyamond
November 2015

HYPOCRITE

Two days later, you called your brother to come to LA from Las Vegas. When he rang the doorbell, grandma nor I was expecting him, but we knew something was up. My cousin Mel didn't like the vibe and asked me to come stay with him at his mom's crib that night. I told him I'd be fine, "Ain't shit finna happen to me". I stayed in my room until the next day when I had to get up and get ready for work. The next morning, I got into the shower and went into my room to quickly get dressed. Before I could go back into my bathroom to finish my hair, you ran in there and was just sitting around, who knows. I went into grandma's room and asked her if she could get my hair products out the restroom for me because I was trying to avoid confrontation.

When grandma asked me if I was going to speak to my uncle, I told her *no*, right in front of his face. His energy was nothing to even acknowledge if you asked me. He came for confrontation; he must have lost his goddamn mind. He then fixed his mouth to speak and said "See, why she can't ever do shit for herself?" and of course I answered back "Shut yo fat ass up" and then we began to argue. When he told me not to speak to him until I can talk to him with respect, I asked him why he thought I didn't speak in the first place? I told him to look at himself. How could I respect him, when he doesn't even respect himself? When I walked back to my room, he was still yelling from my grandma's room. He yelled, "You tryna get over on my grandma" and when I yelled back "But you still getting checks from my grandma" it must've hit a nerve for him because he got his fat ass up and walked to my bedroom.

He stepped towards my doorway and told me I better shut the fuck up and when I told him I dared him to touch me, he chopped me in my motherfucking throat. If I had ever been afraid of a 300-400-pound nigga, best believe all that fear went out the window because I socked that nigga so hard his glasses flew off his fat ass head into the bathroom. And then you came. You came flying out the bathroom and jumped right in swinging. Yelling "You not gonna do that in front of my grandma". But I didn't fight back because I was too busy trying to protect my stomach. I curled up and wouldn't let go of your hair until grandma told us to stop if she even told us to stop. I just remember you yelling, "let go of my hair" which I didn't really want to. I should've pulled it all out like you did me when I was in the 7th grade huh?

Anyhow... you and your brother left my bedroom and I told y'all I was calling the police. I was appalled that this fat ass nigga touched me while I was carrying a baby, his niece and your granddaughter. Fucking trifling. When I grabbed my phone, you ran back in my bedroom and fought me for my phone, saying "You not about to call the police on my brother". When you got ahold of it, you went into grandma room where I ran up on you. We fought in her room for however long while she watched. Punching you in your head, but it wasn't hard enough because you tried to swing my head into the wall, just like you did in the 7th grade. But this wasn't 7th grade, all my nails broke on your head and you still ain't give me my phone back. I walked out grandma's room and went back into mine to grab my other phone and still called the police on y'all.

While I waited for them to arrive, your brother left then figured out that probably wasn't a good idea, so he came back. And you came outside to harass me. You told me "Oh I let my demons consume me, you're the real demon!!" and you didn't stop there. You said all kind of shit. When the police finally came, I told them what happened and then they went inside to talk to you, grandma and your brother. Whatever y'all must've said they believed because they disregarded the scratches on my face, my bloody lip and my pregnant belly and tried to ask me to calm down as if it were some misunderstanding. I told them I wanted my phone back and they got it from you, then left.

Filled with anger and pain, I left too. I went to pick up my father so he could come get all my shit out of the house. I was distraught, most of all, betrayed by my own grandmother, while I was carrying her great-great-granddaughter. I was truly in disbelief. My grandma didn't see me or hear from me for 2 days. Crying to everybody that she regrets what she had allowed. It took my grandma's sister to get me to come home and she was also the one to kick you out because my grandma didn't have it in her to do so.

She said you had some nerve because she used to get calls from the neighbors about boys sneaking out your bedroom window and that was before my father. She called you a hypocrite because you laid up with my 20-year-old father when you were 16 years old and made a baby in her sister's house. A baby neither one of y'all even took much care of.

You showed up to the house on multiple occasions to visit grandma. When my daughter was 2 months old, I felt remorseful and put her in your arms. I watched your face light up as you held your granddaughter. You never even apologized for attacking me while I was pregnant with her, but I loved you enough to forgive you on my own and allowed you to fall in love with my daughter.

CUT ME DEEP

I remember the argument like yesterday.
Something came on the radio and you and your homegirl
started politicking in the front seat about how my generation is
disrespectful and crazy.
When I finally got tired of hearing y'all old asses subliminally
talk shit,
I turned to look at Brandee and yelled "Y'all calling us
disrespectful and crazy, but y'all are the quote unquote ones who
raised us and y'all crack babies".
READ.

And you dead ass responded with "At least I don't cut myself".
READ FOR FILTH.

That shit cut me deeper than any blade I've ever put to my
skin...
THAT SHIT CUT ME DEEP

However, I knew your hate stemmed from me being proud of
who I was.

Dyamond Taylor
Mrs. Gavia
English IV P6
November 9, 2012

Self-Harm

Those who are ignorant to self-harm are typically the ones who make judgement that a person committing the act is doing so solely for the purpose of wanting attention. Yet self-harm has been around for ages and is just now being exposed because mental illness is finally [starting to get took seriously]. People assume that every cut is an attempt to suicide, but if you look closely to a cutter's arm you will see that they have never gone deep enough. Intentions of people who commit self-harm are to hurt themselves rather than anybody around them. After the first wound, they realize they found something more than suicide -- they found an outlet. Whether or not it is healthy, people who commit self-harm do so because they can't [or choose not to] handle the emotional pain they endure. Self-harm is just one of many forms of escapism.

Although, I can't justify the behavior, I will educate one on the means of the act. "Some kind of event in their lives that has been very difficult to process and it has left emotional scars", when a person feels that they have no control over the issues surrounding them or more importantly how their emotions have caused them to react, they attempt to take control the only way they feel they can (Kennedy). "By injuring, the pain [they once had no control over] now becomes visible and tangible" (Styer). This act of injury is the only way "they know how to clean a wound" which helps them feel like they've gained back control (Styer). Thus, symbolizing what is hurting them because a person might find it impossible to let go of the pain since they do not know how to even take the step of acknowledging it. "Representing the capacity to feel worthy of happiness and be able to successfully address life challenges..." that is of course when one is ready (Auden). As opposed to their emotional pain lingering, being a constant reminder to them of the hurt in which they suffer from daily, "I cut because it was the one time that I had control of where I hurt, how bad it felt and whether or not it left a scar" (Snow qtd in Schodolski). One can only hold in their emotions for so long until they find that release, that they have been yearning for.

Evidently hypersensitive and often selfless, one will steer away from hurting others which will result in inflicting that pain to him or herself. When actions aren't honest and lead to hurt, a person will take out their anger and frustration on themselves in order to protect others from being hurt. "What is succorance? Simply put, it is the need to be taken care of, to be loved and succored", some people love too deep to ever hurt the person who is hurting them, ignoring the fact that the person and relationship is toxic because they are codependent (Shneidman). When the love given isn't reciprocated, the person will take out the anger from the pain they hold, on him or herself, as actress Angelina Jolie explained, "So I went through a period of time where I would feel trapped, I'd cut myself because it felt like I was releasing something, and that it was honest" (qtd in Schodolski). Trying so hard to make another person's actions right, they ignore their own health with this coping mechanism.

When the person or people they care about can't fulfill their needs, they search for an escape. The life of a person who inflicts harm to themselves begins to feel like self-harm is the only high they can run to. They become consumed with the burning sensation that runs all throughout their body while everything on their mind fades away and they're are the only ones who can cure and "nurse" that physical pain. Giving themselves what they think is a solution to their problem, a sense of control. "When we cut, tear, or burn our skin, we stimulate nerve endings. When this occurs, endorphins are released from our brain and we experience a high for about 15-20 mins" (Styers). They've found their freedom, "however, when it does become habitual, and they have learned to get rid of their feelings; then they get very numb. They have stuffed those feelings away and now they are left wanting to feel something" and that's when they feel like there is nothing else they can run to (Lader qtd in Kennedy). Hopelessly, blinding him or herself to the positivity in life.

Indeed, a person who loves and respects him or herself would never purposely do anything to harm their self, however when a person loses all hope, "-her hunger for it; her inability to obtain it; her frustration with her unfulfilled need for it; her willingness to die for it", and the void they have within will incite them to live and act in self-indulge (Shneidman). Ironically, causing them to neglect their self-worth, and in the midst, lose the most important thing they didn't know they had, --him or herself.

I once read, "those who self-injure are not "crazy". Based upon my observation they generally tend to be intelligent, creative, very sensitive and caring individuals who express difficulty communicating" (Styer). I used that quote to hence that while many of those who indulge in self-harm are only misunderstood and shamed by society, called "crazy" and often accused of being "attention seekers" and are ignorant to the fact that they can receive help and even scared to ask for help. While it is easy to judge a book by its cover, it is hard to read someone, who is afraid to open up because they often live in shame from the pain society has caused them.

Work Cited

Auden, C. McClure, et al. "Characteristics Associated with Low Self-Esteem among US Adolescents. *Academic Pediatrics* 10.4 (2010): 238, 44. E2. *ProQuest Career and Technical Education; ProQuest Research Library.* Web. 5 Nov. 2012. Kennedy, Angela. "Self-Injury on Rise." *Counseling Today* Vol. 47, No. 5. Oct. 2004: 20+. *SIRS Issues Researcher.* Web. 30 Oct 2012.

Scholdolski, Vincent J. "Self-Injury Cuts Deeper into America's Youth." Chicago Tribune (Chicago, IL). Aug. 8 2005: n.p. *SIRS Issues Researcher.* Web. 02 Nov 2012

Shneidman, Edwins. The Suicidal Mind. New York: Oxford UP, 1996. Print.

Styer, Denise M. "An Understanding of Self-Injury and Suicide." *Prevention Researcher Integrated Research Services, Inc.,* Vol. 13, *Supplement.* Dec. 2006: 10-12 *SIRS Issues Researcher.* Web. 05 Nov 2012.

*Freed*2013

To avoid the hurt that makes me go insane
I do some shit people find strange
because I've fallen in love with self-inflicted pain

Thoughts of suicide all in my daydream
I slit my wrist and let my soul sing
"LET ME FREE" while I can hear my grandma's scream

May have something to do with my dead self-esteem
Probably has everything to do with my parents not wanting me
I don't need to live this scheme called Life with its impossible
"Be Happy" theme

Depression is what makes me cum alive
Depression is what makes me sexy
Depression is what fuels my sex drive

Depression is what opens my body and never keeps me
deprived
My body might die tomorrow but my soul would survive

To make everything construe
I cut through my perfect skin to release my soul that's overdue
and with my loving instrument I slice into what I hope to find a
breakthrough
While I cut myself I let my soul sneak out to speak to me

My skin breaks and my soul flees
We converse a little and people call me crazy
But with cutting, I've made memories
And with blacking out I've come to know me

I am not my body but my soul
and when people are afraid to be themselves
I am the one who holds up my wrist
Bold

Damaged Goods

MY MOMMA AND DADDY LOST ME IN THEIR
DAMAGED TRIAL
CUHS THEY WERE TOO YOUNG TO BREAK THE
CYCLE

YOUNG IN LOVE, INSECURE, AND INDENIAL
NIGHTMARES FROM BOTH THEIR CHILDHOODS
ONLY RECYCLED

I WAS ONLY 8 YEARS OLD WHEN I FIRST STARTED
FEELING SUICIDAL
BECAUSE THEY NEVER BOTHERED TO CHECK IF I
WAS VITAL

MY MOTHER ENTITLED TO HER DREAMS
STARTED THINKING BRIDAL
SHE THEN LOST ME TO THE WILD WHEN SHE
FORGOT ALL ABOUT HER CHILD

DYAMOND IN THE ROUGH

ME, HER, AND MY DADDY NEVER ASKED TO BE PUT
IN THIS BROKEN SOCIETY
ONLY TO GROW DEPENDENT ON EACH OTHER AND
LACK SOBRIETY

MY MOTHER FINALLY LEFT MY FATHER AFTER SO
LONG OF DAMAGING HER PRIDE
MY FATHER BROKE HIS OWN HEART THROUGH HIS
CHEATING AND LIES

I WATCHED BOTH MY PARENTS COMPASSION DIE
WHEN THEY NO LONGER COULD CONFIDE
OR HIDE THEIR LUST INSIDE

MY MOMMA LOST HERSELF AS SOON AS SHE WAS
BETRAYED AT HER WORST
MY DADDY LACKED FIDELITY BECAUSE HE WAS
TOO DAMAGED TO EVER FULLY LOVE HER FIRST

NEVER MATTERED HOW MUCH GOOD WE TRIED TO
PUT IN THIS EARTH
SPITE RAN THROUGH OUR VEINS AS IF WE WERE
CURSED

MOM,
I DON'T JUDGE YOU FOR BELIEVING YOU WERE
RUINED
I KNOW HOW LOSING YOUR MOTHER COULD HAVE
YOU INFLUENCED

A GIRL WHO HAD NOTHING GOT CREATIVE AND
MADE A BABY
YOU HAD ME FOR SECURITY JUST AS YOU ONCE
STATED

DYAMOND IN THE ROUGH

IT DIDN'T MAKE IT ANY BETTER THAT THE NIGGA
YOU PICKED HAD YOUR NOSE WIDE OPEN
ALL THE NAKED FEELINGS YOU CHOSE TO INVEST
JUST FOR THIS NIGGA TO TURN AROUND AND MAKE
IT A CONTEST

HE BROKE YOUR HEART EVEN MORE AND DIDN'T
EVEN HELP CLEAN UP THE MESS
AS IF THE DAMAGED MOTHER OF HIS LOVE CHILD
WAS SECOND BEST

MY DADDY ACTED A FOOL BECAUSE AS A CHILD HE
WAS OPPRESSED
HE LACKED SECURITY BUT WAS TOO PRIDEFUL TO
TELL YOU HE WAS REALLY DEPRESSED

YOU BOTH THOUGHT I'D BE THE CURE TO THE
SAME DISEASE YOU BOTH POSSESSED
BUT Y'ALL ONLY ENDED UP ABANDONING ME IN
THE PROCESS

DAD,
YOU ALWAYS PICKING UP THAT BOTTLE
STILL HURTING BECAUSE YOUR PARENTS
ABANDONED YOU AS A CHILD

YOUR NIGHTMARES FROM YOUR CHILDHOOD ONLY
RECYCLED
A DAMAGED 12-YEAR-OLD BECAUSE OF YOU MY
SOUL WAS SUICIDAL
IRONICALLY INTERRUPTED BECAUSE YOU
PRACTICALLY TRADED YOUR VITALS

YOU DAMAGED YOUR BRAIN FROM ALCOHOLISM
SO HOW COULD YOU EVER HEAL YOUR WOUNDS
UNDER THESE CONDITIONS

111

DYAMOND IN THE ROUGH

WOULD YOU SAY YOU'RE A VICTIM WHOSE PAST
HAS HIM IMPRISONED?

DAMAGED FATHER I BET YOU DIDN'T THINK I'D BE
THE SAME
NOW I SEE YOU IN THE STREETS AND YOU CAN'T
EVEN REMEMBER MY NAME

A HURT PERSON
THAT'S DAMAGED GOODS

CONSISTENT REMINISCENCES OF A FUCKED-UP
CHILDHOOD
I CALL THEM NIGHTMARES FROM PARENTS BEING
MISUNDERSTOOD
NOW I'M 20 YEARS OLD WORTH DAMAGED GOODS

IN LOVING MEMORY

of

ROBINETTE SHIPP FLOYD

Friday, May 8, 1992
2:30 P.M.

Angelus Crenshaw Chapel
3875 Crenshaw Boulevard
Los Angeles, California

Father Patrick Gorman
Officiant

What We Keep In Memory Is Ours Forever

DYAMOND IN THE ROUGH

When I think of my story and the courage I have to speak up, I think of all the people who didn't make it this far to be able to. When y'all see drug addicts, I see undisclosed pain, because I been there. When y'all see homeless people, I see people who got lost in the fear of their full potential, because I been there.

The picture is just so much bigger, but we be too busy looking down on others as if we're any better than them. My mom lost her mother in May of 1992 when she was only 14 years old. She got pregnant with me 2 years later, but I couldn't fill the void she was longing to fill. She needed me to, but I couldn't. My mom has cried every year on Mother's Day since I could remember.

I know there's much more missing from my Grandmommy Robinette's story than what's been told, and I truly wish she was here to share her truth.

One thing I do know is that when our body dies, our souls do not. You feel me? Robinette got that Big Energy. I know that she's the something in me that I feel pushing me hard to have this courage to speak my muthafuckin mind to entitled ass people, never mind how they might feel after. It's her energy inside me giving me the strength to press on and be the greatest-realest version of me. When my aunts and older cousins call me her name by what they think is an accident, it's not.

She is me and I am her.

Ase.

CHAPTER 6

STAINED DYAMONDS

Vanity Slave

I use my makeup brush when I masturbate
Use a spoon whenever I wanna taste
My pussy drips gold cuhs I'm the heavyweight
Shaped perfect like the figure 8
Except I got the slippery slopes
Too dangerous to ever be played
Always anxious for your girl to throw her bouquet
But I ain't ever getting married
Just to stay and lay each day
While he splashes around
Shit
I just wanna play
With my makeup brush
While I masturbate
Got a little juicy
Guess it's time to finger paint
Who would've thought my juice could help me create
I turn to an orgasm to sedate
Cuhs why should I have to wait
I'm openly admitting I'm a vanity slave
Vain in my own sex game
I cater to myself to avoid the pain
Prefer a mirror but I love to watch my shadow play
Saying no thank you to all last names
Masturbating to my own pictures in gold frames
Ain't no shame in my own acclaim
Making love to myself could never change
Can't keep my hands out my pants cuhs I'm enslaved
Just a touch is what keeps the pain away
Many not knowing how to explain
Because they weren't there when I wasn't tamed
All as a little girl I was depraved
Now you see my sex appeal on every page
Congratulations!
You know a Vanity Slave

"DYAMONDDD"

I ran down the first flight of stairs rolling my eyes, then fixed my face as if nothing was wrong as I ran down the last flight.

"Yes, Aunt Nikki."

You told me to sit down because you wanted to ask me something.

"Who touched you?"

Before I could even think you added "– because I was touched, and you act like how I use to."

I thought to myself, do I lie? I held my breath and blurted out a name.
And even though you looked uneasy about the information you'd received, you moved closer to comfort me.
Instead of being able to be present in that moment, I felt numb because of the mental block that held me captive for years.

Nightmares

I see you peepin'
while I'm in and out my dreamin'
Fingerin' me
while you think I'm sleepin'
I make one move to pretend I'm wakin'
and your old ass moves faster than what your fingers were
pacin'
NIGGA YOU NASTY!
And these "Hoes"
because that's what we're called, Right?
Hoes…
These "Hoes" who are "Fast" are forever scarred.
It all started at 3 in the mornin'
when we'd sleep at our grandma's house
Our worlds would suddenly fall apart
He'd wait for everybody to fall asleep to violate our sacred
body parts
He touched my adolescent body while I laid there awake
Terrified, I was having a bad dream with the devil and his
snakes
A nightmare that would never go away
Too scared to let that nasty ass old nigga know I had heart
Too scared to break a cycle I knew nothing about nor didn't
start

NASTY ASS OLD NIGGAZ DRAGGING INNOCENT
YOUNG GIRLS INTO THE DARK.

Dyamond in the Rough Guidance Center

PROGRESS NOTE

Appt. Date: 12/20/11

Start Time: 2:00pm **Participants:** Patient

Description of session, including behavioral obeservations and response to treatment:

She said the med (Seroquel) does help her not have nightmares but makes her tired all day. Thx challenged her thought processes but pt was insistent on being negative and pessimistic today.

Assessment of progress in treatment and current functioning:
Pt's mood has been depressed and her thought process was very negative. She denied SI/HI and said she is just focused on her future and feeling hopeful when she is on her own

Stop Time: 2:50pm

Confessional

I've questioned whether or not, I blocked out the thoughts in my head for so long to protect you? You'd been my best friend since I was born, you were all I knew. It wasn't until after you passed away that I acknowledge the pain you caused me. Internal confusion hit when I finally had the courage to ask God why you did what you did and exactly how many times had you might have done it to me.

I then began to resent you. All the good memories started to fade when coming across pictures of you holding me as an infant. You would think I'd miss the man who raised me... Instead, my own thoughts just haunt and taunt me. Flashbacks of the night I caught you touching me, imagining you changing my diaper. This is the type of shit I let eat me up on the inside from age 18-22 and I started to resent my other best friend who raised me too, Grandma.

Many disputes often came about, especially when I wanted to do things my way. Grandma would often tell me I needed to follow the laws and rules because you were a sheriff. She'd often throw in my face that you were a "saint" and jokingly joke that you'd be turning over in your grave if you saw or heard what I was doing. I would snap and tell her that I don't give fuck right in her face. I'll admit it always hurt to see how shocked she'd look at me. She'd then asked, "You don't care about Daddy?" Oh mah gawd, hearing her called you that made me cringe.

"–The man who gave us everything we have?" Yep the nigga who took everything I had away.

I would burst into complete anger and tell her to shut up and continue to cringe at her gloat of you. She'd look at me crushed like I was just a disrespectful teenager, then go silent. Which ultimately silenced my painful truth. I was trapped in my own shame.

I soon started to resent her since I couldn't tell her what you did to me. I just knew if she'd believed me it would break her heart and I knew if she didn't believe me, I would die from an overdue broken soul.

Over the years she'd go so far to express her hate and disgust for my Papa Andre, who was a pimp, but little did she know it was her own husband, a retired sheriff, a "saint", the man she worshipped who'd vandalized my innocent soul. You damaged my trust worse than any man on this Earth, including my father who abandoned me and left me with you.

On the day, my mother and her 300-pound brother attacked me while I was 4 months pregnant, it was my grandma, the one who saved me most of my life, who told the police that I was crazy. And when I asked her why she lied to the police, she told me because she didn't want to embarrass your name.

She lied on me, to protect you…

On January 25th, 2018

My grandmother and I were watching Larry Nassar's trial on the news and she was curious as to why the girls waited so long to report him, so I told her about this time I got sexually assaulted by a porn star when I was 19. I explained to her how he tricked me into thinking he was a photographer that wanted to shoot me. She asked me if I ever went to the police and I told her no. Then she asked me why not with this puzzled look on her face. I told her because even though I never watched porn to know who this man was, I felt so stupid and naive for putting myself in the position to even be sexually assaulted. I told her I blamed myself and assumed the police would too. When she gave me this sympathetic look, it was then with tears in my eyes, I could no longer keep in the shame I'd been allowing to eat me alive all these years. I told her I'd been touched when I was a child by a family member, and she was very eager to find out who. We even played the guessing game... but she never guessed who. I finally had the courage to tell the most important person in my life, my biggest secret that had been eating me alive since I was 14 years old. I was scared but ready– ready to be free, ready to move on with my life.

I explained why it took me so long to gain the courage to tell her and she understood. She looked at me so unsettling and proceeded to tell me "I'm sorry baby, that's terrible...You're right you probably would've put a wedge in the family, and they would've talked about it for years and downed you like nobody's business".

Although I was very relieved that she took me in with love and understanding. I thought to myself, who gives a fuck about my family downing me? Maybe if I had been vocal about what happened to me, there would've been a chance I could've saved myself from the pain I came to struggle with for years.

A prime example today, on why young girls are afraid to speak up about being sexually abused. We weren't ever the 'Huxtables', so what more damage could it have done? I was the one who had to suffer the consequences and I did so all by myself. I wore that humiliation underneath all my clothes, in the pit of my soul. Beating myself to forget what vivid memories haunt me in my dreams.

Trapped in fear of becoming an outcast in my own family because I could never be sure if they would have accepted my reality.

Not once had I seen anybody in my family help embrace another's pain unless it involved death. I listened to these people put my mother and father down for years, as I grew up. There was nothing more devastating than being abused and having to live with it in silence because I was mortified that I'd be crucified by my own family for speaking up and telling the truth. Even as a little girl, I could feel that what had happened to me was shameful. And even as a little girl, I allowed my anxiety of getting rejected to silence me. I'd been torn in pieces since the day I caught him in the act because who was teeny tiny me to throw away a bond of more than 60 years. Do you know how many times I thought I had the courage to speak up, only to break down and bite my tongue.

Just thinking about it pulls at my heartstrings.

DYAMOND IN THE ROUGH

I was 19 years old when I got a job at the Slauson Swap Mall selling local rapper's merchandise. One day in April, a man walked up to my booth and started complimenting me on my "natural beauty". He made it a point to emphasize how much he loved the fact that I didn't wear any makeup or acrylic nails.

After showering me with so many compliments, he proceeds to ask me if I was a model. He then pulled out a wad of cash, along with a business card that read "Mike's Hot Video Girls" and told me he was a photographer. He asked me if I was available to shoot the next day and I naively agreed. I mean I was 19 and this nigga had a business card, so I thought he was legit.

He told me he'd pick me up and was really specific about what he wanted me to wear. A crop top and some leggings while remaining adamant about no makeup. Real basic, so he couldn't be a predator, right? Well, predators come in many different forms masked with professional occupations amongst hidden spaces.

The day of the shoot, he called me to tell me he was outside. But to my surprise when I ran out to meet him, he was sitting in a busted ass bucket. As soon as I opened the door to get in, I was greeted with the back-facing camera on his iPhone recording me. I didn't know what the fuck was going on, so of course, I had this dumb ass smile on my face trying to cover up my confusion.

As we got closer to the freeway, I glanced at his backseat and discovered several X-rated DVDs. I immediately turned back to the front and let it be known that I didn't do porn so he shouldn't waste his time or gas if that was his expectations for this photoshoot. He laughed nonchalantly and reassured me that we'd only be taking still photos, so I agreed to continue on with the shoot.

As we got farther away from my house, he told me to grab a few DVDs from the back. He then pointed to certain keywords asking me to read them out loud such as "amateur" and "first timer". I told him that it was cool and all but reiterated that I didn't do porn.

After driving for some time, I looked up and notice that we were all the way in the Valley. I remember walking into an apartment complex and getting on an elevator as I started to analyze this nigga— the wife beater, dramatic fake ass jewelry, and muscular steroid-like

124

stature. I told him he looked like he did porn and he laughed while fixing his muthafuckin mouth to request that I say it again... on his iPhone camera.

When we walked out the elevator to what I thought would be his apartment or studio, I soon realized that this nigga was breaking into the gym and that is when all optimism flew out the fuckin window. My naivety up until this point had me feeling foolish, but I tried to play it cool while forcing an awkward smile. I was all the way in the valley so what else was my dumb ass supposed to do?

My guy pulled out a release form and a pen for me to sign for our quote-unquote photoshoot then asked me for my id so he could take a picture of it. And so the foolishness began...

I should've known he was on some weird shit, directing me to pose without a professional camera in sight. He told me to turn around, face the wall, and arch my back "a little". Out of nowhere, I felt my pants being forced down and a wet tongue stabbing my coochie, all while he recorded himself doing so.

Shit happened so fast and for a moment it felt as if time froze. My body stiffened as I felt him repeatedly moving his tongue, violating me. Quickly snapping back to reality, I realized what was happening with my phone still in my hand. I frantically texted my cousin "Bro this nigga eating me out on camera" and she responded back immediately saying "Bro a porn star now?". Before I could even text her back, I pushed his big ass off me.

I was disgusted, but more afraid than anything. For the third time, I told this nigga that I did not do porn– this time with tear filled eyes. He then goes on to beg me to make a sex scene with him for a thousand dollars. No matter how many times I rejected his advances, he continuously tried to manipulate and guilt trip me into complying with his fucked up reverse psychology.

The first time I said no, he asked if it was because I thought he was ugly. The second time I said no, the nigga attempted to degrade me by throwing in my face that "I already do it for free", yet all I could think was those previous encounters were consensual. The third time I said no, I told him I was mentally ill and this weak ass nigga had the audacity to say "Why? You're a beautiful girl" as if he didn't just fucking sexually assault me.

I told that nigga right then and there I might go home and kill myself after this shit, so if the sex scene he wanted was a thousand, that nigga owe me five for licking my coochie without permission. Periodt. For 30 minutes we went back and forth, with me telling this nigga to take me home. When I told him, I would wait outside and have my cousin come get me, he finally gave in and took me back to the crib.

We pulled up to my house and he went on to tell me that I was an evil little girl. As I walked to my front door ashamed of what I had almost gotten my dumb ass into, I never felt safer to be home. When I got inside, I grabbed my car key and told my cousin to ride with me to the park. I parked in a secluded space, turned up my car's volume, and told my cousin to listen to this shit…

3 disturbing voice memos
and this bitch only replied, *"Was that Brian Pumper?"*

Hell no I didn't go to the police.
Humiliation was an understatement.
Everybody knew this nigga was a predator, but me.

DYAMOND IN THE ROUGH MEDICAL OFFICE

Taylor, Dyamond L
MRN:
DOB: 11/3/1994, Sex. F

History of Sexual Assault

Patient reports that she was molested several times by her great grandfather (a retired sheriff) when she was a little girl.

Patients reports that she was raped by a boyfriend of 3 years when she tried to leave him at the age of 18.

Patient reports that she took a modeling job and was manipulated by a photographer who was actually trying to get her involved in a pornography video.

Patients reports that she never disclosed or processed any of these issues

Lady in a Glass Dress

Many have come into my life with pure intent to make sure
they'd take a piece of me with them when they'd leave,
which they all did.
They opened me up just to invade my privacy, scheming to rob
then extort me...
It was all a game to them, plotting to get comfortable
until I exposed myself.
I allow each and every one to see right through me.
Lady in a Glass Dress
I called myself.
I did it each time with each person.
It was like I was trying to find a cure.
You know that feeling when you are completely empty,
you depend on life to fill your cup and let that shit run over?
All the nothingness in my heart would mate with my brain and
leave me vacant.
My heart craved to see the good in each person
but everyone I exposed my raw self to raped me,

figuratively speaking.

I allowed my insides to become tainted by this society
I saw beauty in.
Written on my open soul each time, "Abuse Me, Destroy Me"
and they did.
Tore me apart just to see what was inside,
fed off me and appropriated a piece of me just to supply air to
their ego.
Naive of me to not want to believe people could actually be as
greedy as they are
yet the more I let these demons in, the more my soul drowned
in hell.

DYAMOND IN THE ROUGH

They say the devil is in the details
and if you're not familiar with the idiom it's used for saying
that
something may seem simple, but in fact the details are
complicated and likely to cause trouble.
And trouble is naturally exposed.

When my first devil began to do things to me as a young girl, it
seemed simple.
I was confused and didn't understand what was going on
while he was taking advantage of my innocence
and I didn't do nothing about it.

Oblivious
as to how I could save myself.
Now I'm left to live with the corruption I was injected with
and I blame myself.
Because I wanted those, I had let in to fix me,
but they only saw me for my damaged goods.
Any person I let in to love me, did.
They loved each second of my time they played with.
Loved to watch me open my heart and unclothe my entire
being
just to bleed me.

Demons in human form coveted me time after time
and I continuously chose lust over love.
Blinded by the fear of being alone
I allowed myself to become infected.
I was robbed of my honesty, habitually.
And just like my first demon, the last one hurt just as much.

He came in a form I had not ran into yet
and my fixed pain only nourished my stigma

to let him in because I was too weak to fade temptation.
A temptation that felt so good
and hurt so bad when it was all said and done.

I felt the oxygen leave my lungs as my veins became polluted
with lust.
A disease of wanting everyone I tried to love
to love me
was killing me.

Throwing myself in a pit of fire each time
until I was numb to the feeling of being burned.

Hurting so much
that the pain became
addicting.

[Self-Destruct]

CHAPTER 7

Star Light, Star Bright
My Dyamond Will Shine Tonight

A letter from Grandma:

*I still remember the smell of yellow roses in the hospital room
that your Aunt Nikki sent.*

*Anxiously, I awaited your presence,
I was so excited that I was going to be a great grandmother.
I couldn't wait for all the fun we were going to have together.*

*You have arrived
and of course, your name is Dyamond.*

*So little, so helpless, so beautiful, just like a diamond in the
sky.*

*God's given your mother and father a perfect baby,
but they were too young to raise you.
There was a lot of confusion, neglect and misfortunes.*

*As much as I tried with all my heart to be there for you,
there were times I couldn't.
I just hoped God was listening.*

*I don't even know how you did it for all the time you did, but I
must say you've always been a person of strong character.*

Not Enough *Credit*

You don't get enough credit for raising my mother and her
brother while your daughter didn't and couldn't.
You don't get enough credit for raising my dad from the
moment he was brought in your home.

You let them have me when they asked if they could.
Because you knew I'd be yours.
You don't get enough credit for raising me.

You taught me how to write, and how to add and subtract.
You taught me how to paint, and how to garden.
You don't get enough credit for raising me.

You taught me not to cry over spilled milk or broken dishes.
When I came home crying and told you the boys at school
made fun of my cleft chin,
you would tell me "Michael Jackson paid to have a chin like
yours honey!"
You taught me that I was beautiful and had the perfect
cheekbones.
You don't get enough credit for raising me.

You let me sleep in your bed when I was too scared to sleep
downstairs by myself.
You read me bedtime stories when it was time to go to sleep
and if you weren't reading them, you made them up.
You scratched my back, stomach, arms and even my legs when
I couldn't sleep.
You don't get enough credit for raising me.

You woke me up every morning and help me get ready.
When we'd get to my school, I would duck my head under the
dashboard because I was embarrassed that you were white, you'd
pull up further, so I'd feel comfortable enough to get out the car.
Looking back now, I am embarrassed.

133

DYAMOND IN THE ROUGH

Ashamed of how I could ever be ashamed of having a white
grandma.
Because YOU my dear? White grandma and all? Held it down.
You don't get enough credit for raising me.

And I love you for never allowing me and my 4th-grade
insecurities to hurt your feelings.

You bought me every birthday and Christmas present since I
was born but let my mother write her name on the tags.
You bought me all my school clothes and let my mother take
credit for doing so.
You don't get enough credit for RAISING ME!
You raised me and probably would've let my mother take
credit,
but I would never allow that.
You don't get enough credit for raising me.
When I moved in with my mother and her husband, you'd
always pick up the phone to listen to me cry.
When I called and begged you to come pick me up the next
day, you would call her and let her know you were coming to get
me, as if it were your idea.
When school let out, you'd be waiting right on the corner with
your cowboy hat on.
I'd walk right past you because I was embarrassed, but deep
down inside I would be smiling because I was so happy that you
came to save me.
You never, not even once forgot about me.
You always heard me and listened.
You don't get enough credit for raising me.

You sent me to go live in Texas when you realized my mother
was unfit and you were too far to help me.
When I was frustrated and angry, you'd always pick up the
phone to listen to me cry.
You sent me letters and boxes of gifts while I was 1,400 miles
away.

DYAMOND IN THE ROUGH

You don't get enough credit for raising me.

When I started cutting myself, you cried and begged me not to.
When Aunt Nikki started getting sicker you came and visited
me and help me take care of her.
You cooked us dinner every night and kept me company.
You don't get enough credit for raising me.

You allowed me to be myself around you, you allowed me to
be my wild self around you.
You came to my high school graduation 1,400 miles away.
You felt accomplished and proud when you watched me cross
that stage.
I did it because of you.
You don't get enough credit for raising me.

You spoiled me to a point of no return.
You gave me anything I ever asked for and more.
You loved me with your whole heart.
You don't get enough credit for raising me.

I'm so grateful God blessed me with a great grandmother like
you.
White and all. You held it down. You held me down for 23
years and I know you will never stop.
You don't get enough credit for raising me.

Soulmate

They say once you lose your soulmate you die too
So, when you leave me
Am I supposed to leave everything so I can be with you

Because I don't ever want to forget your soft kisses
From waking me up to greeting me at the door
There are so many things I'll be missing

Our connection so deep
Never had to speak to be able to listen
I been with you for 20 years
and all of a sudden
I hear you feel like quitting

Used to call me a 'Poor Ass'
But I kept these poems flowing
I was the quitter
And you were the one who kept me going

Made my life sweeter in every way possible
Just like when I was little
you never told me no to having a popsicle

Now every time I walk in the house and see you sleeping
I sneak in your room
to make sure you still breathing

My world stops every time I picture you leaving
And my heart drops every time I see you down for any reason

I know my future has appeared unclear
But you've always held me without fear
You've been my #1 supporter who believed in me
when I said writing would be my career

DYAMOND IN THE ROUGH

So grateful you were able to watch me grow
My life has been a storm while you've always been my
rainbow
Dear Grandma, I promise to always help you stand tall
as long as you promise to never let me go

January 2014

Dear Dyme,
Let's get this last letter done.

When you lay in bed at night the best things that you should've said come to mind, as they're supposed to when you're sitting right in front of the person. Not that it justifies it, but maybe if he was never molested, it would've never happened to you my dear. If I would've known, I would've put an immediate stop to it and exposed him, but this letter isn't about him, this letter is about You.

Although I have many regrets, I am so proud of you for coming forward. I wish you would've came forward years ago when it happened. No little girl should have to go through being molested by her grandfather. No little girl should have to go through anything you had to go through as a child.

I pray any teenage girls and women who are reading your story find it a little bit easier to come out to live with their truths. There is help for all sex crime victims and I hope you have shined light on that. You have far more potential than what I've ever imagined.

I got the message and I hope others do too. I love you and I'm sorry this happen to you, but I'm very proud of you for putting it out so that you could help others.

Grandma Jean

July 23, 2018
Star Light Star Bright My Dyamond Will Shine Tonight!

CHAPTER 8

SHEDDING LAYERS

2018

To *him*:

It was 5 years ago that you made the mistake you made and 4 years ago when you texted me an apology. I texted you back that day that I forgave you, but truthfully, I wasn't anywhere near ready to talk about it. So, I just brushed it off not realizing that I didn't really know exactly what you were apologizing for.

When I did decide I was ready to tell my truth, I tried to do so all by myself. I spent more than 10 hours looking for the right words and trying to remember everything I had once worked so hard to forget. As I wrote it all out on paper, memories of me and you were thrown in my own face. When I thought I was finished, I found myself shaking and hovering over my toilet, throwing up nothing. I felt my conscience tell me that it wasn't just my truth I was telling, but yours as well. Once I relived all that I could remember I was afraid. Afraid of how the world would see us both. My own mind started playing tricks on myself to the point where I was now doubting myself, thinking maybe I was just "victimizing" myself. I was in the middle of an anxiety attack when I desperately texted you that I needed your help. I was nervous as fuck for your response, but I still took the chance to reach out to you because I knew I couldn't tell our story without you. I just wouldn't feel right putting out my truth if our stories didn't add up.

When it came time for us to relive it, you were right in front of me and more than willing. I watched you play it cool until helplessly, your emotions invaded your front. As you started to reminisce in how we fell in love, you said to me "I don't know about you, but to me, there was some euphoria in there, like nothing could go wrong– pure happiness". When you started opening up to me about all your cheating, telling me things I'd never known, reminding me of all my self-hate, you started to confirm most of my memories I tried to allow to fade. Reflecting out loud on how you were immature and calling yourself stupid. You couldn't wait to mention the part where I fucked your best friend and even then, I felt no remorse.

I couldn't help, but to start dwelling when we made our way towards the end of our relationship. Although the end of our relationship was the shortest, it sure felt like the longest. I somehow felt how uneasy your energy shifted and we hadn't even started. When we did jump into it, we both confirmed all physical abuse we could remember in full detail. I took responsibility for the first time being my doing. While you were embarrassed to say the rest of the times were you. We both had shame on our face to the point where neither of us looked up at each other because we knew we were wrong. There was no doubt in my heart that we both regret that our relationship had even got to that point.

I felt myself go numb when it was time to talk about what happened on the last day of our relationship. You, however, appeared to be the complete opposite. When I looked you in your eyes and asked you if you were ready to tell me what you remembered from that day, you cringed and said yes. You told me the beginning, detail for detail as I watched you become more transparent at that moment. Hurt from hearing your own words, I found you stuck in your own thoughts. 5 years later, you are still traumatized because you allowed your demons to consume you. You took a deep breath and I could feel the humiliation fill the room as you were about to reveal what you did to me. I couldn't take it anymore. I saw all my pain and yours when I looked back in your eyes and I stopped you. I told you that you didn't have to tell me because I actually remember that part vividly. You left my house destroyed, having to accept that the bad outweighed the good in our relationship.

You can see now, why I couldn't tell our truth by myself. A lot of the shit we went through was too just too painful for me to want to believe really happened, especially at my age. I tried to force myself to forget all of the painful memories, but they somehow were and still are the ones that haunt me like nightmares. As for the good memories, they've all most likely disappeared. And as much as I knew and hated that our story would be conflicting, I knew you would be one of the few to understand. Possibly risking everything you have because you know how much telling my whole story meant to me. I can't express how grateful I am that you allowed me to call you when I was ready to set myself free. I hope knowing that I genuinely forgive you, can set your soul free too. It took so much courage to be able to tell my story and I know it took just as much courage for you to be the man to help me embrace our truth.

Truthfully, it was extremely brave of you to come over my house to help me tell our kid love story. And I say brave because there are so many boys/ "men" who go through their whole life not only not acknowledging their mistakes, but also never even realizing what mistakes they actually made. So many boys/ "men" who are too sick in their own ideal of masculinity that are too toxic or afraid to apologize. So many who don't care about how much the women/girls who loved or trusted in them were left scarred and damaged from the pain and trauma they caused. There are probably many boys/ "men" who think it's too late to apologize for the mistakes they made when they were younger.

BUT NOT YOU.

You never lied
You took responsibility and acknowledged my pain
You didn't pressure me into minimizing my trauma
You let me heal on my own time
You believed in me and helped me

So, I thank you.

A Letter from *Him*

To the Only Skeleton in My Closet,
   Our relationship was many things, at its foundation it was a lesson. I know your life itself has been a consistent cycle of hard lessons... Our chapter wasn't any different.
I'm sorry, yet grateful to have gone through that lesson with you.
   We were young, not even knowing how to love ourselves, tried time after time to love each other. Without a doubt, our love was real at its peak, but unaware that we still needed self-growth, it tore us apart.
   I've finally reached the point in life to have learned from it all. I pray you too, have grown/learned from the troubles and trauma of our past. I'm here if you need anything.

-Old Lover

2018

To My Dearest Mother,

When I often reflect on all the resentment that manifested in my heart over the many years, I can always count on a flashback from 2015 to project not only in my mind, but heavily on my heart. My father had always stuck up for you, especially when I dogged you but this time, I was pregnant and the feeling I felt stuck with me. He told me I should be easy on you while he proceeded to tell me the story of how Grandmommy Robinette tried to sell you for heroin and that shit really opened my eyes. Not because it was some fucked up shit, but really because it just showed me that I didn't know anything you've really gone through, other than Grandmommy being on heroin most of your childhood.

I don't know how many times I've watched you cry over not having a mother present, but I know my resentment towards you made me feel heartless. All I could think was that I didn't have a mother either and I wasn't sitting here crying. I never even thought about how much or how many times you possibly cried when you were a young girl. It never occurred to me that you probably grew up in denial because you didn't want to remember your mother for all the pain she caused you while she was here. You were 14 years old when she left you here on this Earth with no closure, just her demons. It never occurred to me that you could be more fucked up than me.

I assumed because I lost my Aunt Nikki and had to keep going on with my life, that you were just victimizing yourself. I had to reflect on the days where I too, woke up and cried. So, who am I to judge you for crying over not having a mother on Mother's Day, even though you made it to where I felt like I didn't have one either?

Instead of ever acknowledging and apologizing for the mistakes you made and pain you caused, you just tried to justify them by telling me that parenting didn't come with a manual. That would only add insult to injury for me because at that point you were supposed to create your own manual. You'd tell me each time "You keep bringing it up...you wasn't the only one who was traumatized". You've insisted that you're over your past and just want to focus on the future. You made me think to myself "Am I crazy?" because you want credit for raising me, but don't want to take responsibility for any of the mental abuse or trauma you've caused. I've had to battle myself to forgive you ever since I could remember. Every time I would let you back in, wishing I'd get an apology or even an explanation. I would've died for you to change, but you couldn't help but show me that nothing would ever change.

I have to sit here and wonder if I'm crazy because you've never grasped the pain you've put me through, because of the pain you've been in for so long. When I first read 'Damaged Goods' to you back in 2014, I was so proud of that piece and you gave me the stalest look. I asked you if you liked it, and you told me no. My feelings got hurt because for the first time I put myself in your shoes and stuck up for you. I told the truth about you and my father.

One more thing, since my daughter was born people have told me "She's gonna be prettier than you when she gets older" which left me to wonder who even thinks to joke like that? When people don't know what sense of self-worth anybody has. I really can't imagine how much you probably heard that bullshit. I can't imagine what you felt, after all the pain your mother and father put you through. To add fuel to the fire, the pain my dad put you through that might've made you feel less than the woman you are. And these ol' shallow muthafuckas are trying joke about how I'm going to be prettier than you. I'm the one who had to grow up with that hurt and subtle resentment. I had to grow up with the self-hate you probably didn't even know you passed down to me.

All I ever wanted was for you to simply embrace who you are because you are beautiful in my eyes and always have been. I remember when I was a little girl and you'd be getting ready to go out, I'd watch you put on your brown lipstick. After you'd leave, I'd go in the bathroom and put it on. That memory takes me back to loving you. My daughter takes me back to loving you from her loving me. If it were up to me, I'd love you the same.

And I never meant to add any more pain to all the suffering you had to endure. I sat and thought about all the many years, I chose my father's side over yours. All the years I thought to myself I loved my daddy more when he wasn't even there. That shit wasn't right, but I was just a little girl and y'all were still kids too.

I don't think I've ever even thanked you for always being the one to hold my head high up and wipe my tears for me every time my dad failed me. I don't think I've ever thanked you for picking me up that day he had his first seizure right in front of my eyes and comforting me. So thank you Mommy, I love you.

I just want my truths to open the door for you to tell yours and not be ashamed of who you are. To not be afraid to relive what happened to you because it's time you set yourself free from all the pain you survived. Fuck who you were, my heart and soul tell me YOU ARE STRONG, and you deserve all the help you can get because I know you're tired of fighting this lifelong battle with depression. I just want you to embrace who you are, so you can see how many women you inspire. See how many other women embrace you, as they feel the courage to set themselves free as well.

LOVE YOURSELF
AND LIVE YOUR TRUTHS.

HAPPY MOTHER'S DAY
2018

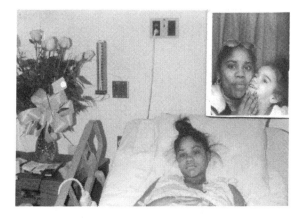

Dear Ladybug (Dyamond),

Once you closed the hole in my heart, I knew I had to stop being a cry baby over my mommy's death and be your mother to carry on her legacy. At the end of every day I never wanted to see you hurt, I just to see you succeed. I want you know to as a mother, you don't ever want your baby/babies to be harmed or in any pain. If any pain comes to your child, you wanna take it away from them. Babe, as much as we go and been through, just know I want to take the pain and disappointment away. I'm sorry for the way I made you feel; we both were traumatized. We will move forward and build a stronger bond, so you can carry on the legacy. I learn something new from you every time we talk. I hope in releasing this work of art, you find all the closure and healing you need to help yourself evolve into the woman you want to be. We might agree and disagree on things, but forever in eternity you are my heart. Mommy will always love her ladybug.

2019

Heal
Your
Inner
Feminine
By
Forgiving
Your
Mother
For
The
Times
She
Let
Her
Own
Pain
Manifest
Into
Yours.

-Cindy Official

Day by Day

My dad got out of jail at 3 am on Saturday, June 1st but my spirit wasn't moved in the slightest at his release. When I called my Papa Andre's phone, my dad picked up sounding too giddy, and I immediately questioned it and became irritated. When they picked me up from KRST at 11 in the morning, I genuinely found myself having to ask them if they had a drink that morning. Papa Andre told me he didn't drink and drive and my dad said no, that he was "just high off life".

So, at that point, I was just trying to figure out why everybody was so happy. I asked Papa Andre if he wanted to buy me breakfast from Fred's and he said "Of course, I'll buy everybody breakfast. We're celebrating." I thought… what are we celebrating? My dad wasn't an innocent man who got locked up for a crime he didn't do. He for sure didn't just get home from doing a bid.

Once my Papa Andre removed himself from our presence, I asked my dad what his plan was (I know some of you certain dumb asses are thinking he just got out of jail blah blah blah... NO my nigga had 14 whole months to read some books and come up with a fuckin plan to better himself) — he said to go home and take a nap... I then told him I was asking about the rest of his life not his day, he tells me he's gonna get a job, which will be extremely hard for him with what he just got a felony for, so I took it as delusion. Two— when I asked him about his goals for his sobriety, he shrugged it off and said "Dyme— I don't know... I'ma take it day by day... I just want to be free"

I don't know. I don't know. I don't know. Between the irritation, I heard in my name when he said it and that fucking "I don't know", I decided I wouldn't be along for the ride this time because how can I truly ride for somebody who doesn't even believe in themselves. When he said he just wanted to be free... I thought... Nigga you could've been free, it's your mentality that has you enslaved!! It's that drank and them drugs that have you enslaved... how can you tell me you just want to be free...

DYAMOND IN THE ROUGH

How about instead of work, you get the proper help you need. How about going to rehab? All this pride to want to get a job, you can't even see the first thing you need to do is get help.

A piece of me died that day as I hopped out another moving car once again and started walking up Crenshaw. All my father could do was open his door halfway and say "Dyamond I love you". He couldn't even hop out and chase me like I once chased after him as a little girl. He didn't have that fight in himself alone. That was all I needed to refuse to be the only one who suffers from the consequences of his weakness, again.

Let me be the martyr for y'all to understand you don't have to stay with or accept y'all abuser whether it's mental, physical, or in my case, spiritual. I just want all my sisters and brothers to know it's okay to choose yourself first. It's okay to cut off those toxic people, even if it's gonna break your fuckin heart because it's your mother or father. Because sometimes it's those same people who set us back 10 times. And not to be misconstrued...I'm not giving up on my father, I will be loving him from a distance until he can decide to want it for himself. When I said I felt a piece of me die that day, I recognized the positive in that feeling was me about to be reborn as I shed old layers of the cycles from toxic relationships that held me back.

To my father,
Damon Andre Taylor.
I'm sorry you feel so ashamed for not being able to protect and provide for your family
and
one day I hope you wake up and realize that you too,
deserve happiness.

2019

CHAPTER 9

PRESSURE OF LIGHT

Marz

I remember the very passionate night that turned into a long early morning.It was no coincidence that it was my Aunt Nikki's birthday.

I never rushed it, we just made it happen. I prayed on it and got an angel as the result. My daughter was not an accident, for she was meant, and God showed me that. I felt highly blessed when I found out about her, even despite the circumstances. I was extremely grateful God gave me this gift on such a meaningful special day. I worked really hard on staying positive my whole pregnancy because I knew I had to protect her energy and that's exactly what I did.

However, I also knew that when she'd come into this world, she wouldn't be the solution to my depression because she was never the problem. My intentions on having my daughter were never in search of finding happiness. I understood not to expect a new innocent life to fill the empty voids that haunted me since I was a kid. I was trapped in my own depression for so many years, that my own daughter's birth wouldn't keep me happy for long.

I could hear people judging me with comments like "You have a beautiful daughter, what you still acting sad for" and "You have a whole baby and you depressed. Get your life together!" Like having a baby was supposed to make all my previous problems go away. But I must say equally birthing my daughter brought me to a certain extent of peace.

Giving life gave me a sense of what I now had to live for, and it wasn't until I started to witness her personality develop beyond what I ever dreamed of that she became my wake-up call.

I had lived with depression for so long that it was my comfort zone. As a child, I knew nothing about depression or mental illness, but I was lonely and sad. Even when I was having the most fun, I would only feel that happiness temporarily. My sadness would always linger in the back of my mind no matter how distracted I'd try to become.

Depression is like an evil spirit constantly climbing on my back, fiddling with my mind. I eventually became scared to even think about happiness. I was so skeptical that when or if I ever achieved the feeling, it could and would be snatched away from me. I grew up with an impassable guard that I subconsciously put up, thinking I was protecting myself, not realizing that I was ultimately self-destructing.

I look back at some of my old tumblr photos and cringe. I'm not proud of my lack of self-love, however, I am proud I overcame such a dark time in my life. It still hurts me to know I thought I had to hurt myself to feel anything other than the pain I was holding onto inside. I received so many messages about people wanting to know how I hadn't drowned in my trauma, but I DID. Many people seem to be confused as to how I've become so forgiving, but I wasn't always like this. I was a child full of sadness who eventually became a teenager full of anger and rage. I was mad at the whole world and do you know who I took that out on? MYSELF. I hated myself for ending up in another state away from the two people who were supposed to be caring for me.

I called out for help so many times. It was not until I was 20 years old that I finally realized that only I can save myself. I blamed myself for all the trauma I'd endured. Forgiving myself was the first step. The second step was understanding that escapism wasn't going to change anything. So, let me be the one to tell you the blade, that drink, and them pills must go. If it wasn't for my daughter and getting pregnant with her at 20, I'm not sure how long it would've taken my stubborn ass to accept the things that I cannot change. Marz saved my life. When I got pregnant with her, I promised to never hurt myself ever again.

From the day I gave birth to my daughter,
I looked in her eyes and could see my entire being.
My depression made me feel lost in the pain I'd been through
but I knew if I didn't wake the fuck up
that one day I'd look in her eyes and see my very own pain.

So, I asked myself when…
When was I going to get my shit together for my daughter, for
myself?

After everything, I'd ever been through as a child to an adult–
the trauma, the mental, physical, emotional, and sexual
abuse— the betrayal.

I found that I was living in shame.

I was honest as hell to the world, but
scared to tell my truths because I was trapped in my family's
pain

I was the one who taught myself about the damaged cycle.
I experienced the abandonment firsthand and for that I lived in
self-hate,
always questioning my worth.

And for how long was I going to continue to allow myself to
dwell in the past,
knowing I have a beautiful daughter that I need and who needs
me to grow with?

I refused to allow her to go through the same pain I went
through.
I wasn't going to allow my escapism to interrupt my daughter.

I knew I had to get out of LA
So, I decided my daughter and I were moving to Texas.

DYAMOND IN THE ROUGH

I remember laying on the table for my first sonogram. I tried my best to act hard (like usual) and not crack a smile as I heard his heartbeat for the first time.

I know God doesn't make any mistakes so I took this one to the chin like I do the rest of the antics. I tried my hardest to avoid putting my mind, body, and soul through any stress, yet I still felt like I dropped the ball. The doctor told me one of four women have a miscarriage and all I thought was how could I be the one in my four? She told me it wasn't mine or anybody's fault, but my ego fought me over that. The thought of "how did I lose my baby" haunted me, over and over again. Until I chose to let go of my ego and realize this was only divine order. This was all part of the plan for my life. I didn't lose my son; he will forever be with me.

Eye believe in the Sun even when it's not Shynin'

Eye believe in the Universe even when it seems shit's not
alignin'
Eye believe in Myself cuhs eye know these scars don't define
me
Eye have hella light work to do— forgiving and refinin'
Eye been sad all my life and now it's time to stop cryin'
Eye know eye can't blame myself for everything
Cuhs absorbing the blame from my pain ain't never solved
anything
Eye recognize the power in enduring for a night
Cuhs eye found joy while being baptized in my baby boy's
delight
Beyond blessed to have found myself under the pressure of
your light
Even still, I've learned that not even I can possess the
moonlight
Sometimes it's better to observe the blessings hidden in plain
sight
The same blessings that at first glance appear as curses
The same curses that make you question if this life is still even
worth it
Those are the blessings that eventually fill life with purpose
Losing you awakened my soul through the death of my ego
I've lived long enough to know after the storm comes a
rainbow
So eye await the day when our souls reunite
Anticipating the moment that eye can be one with my
Sunshyne

Eye love you Eternally.

CHAPTER 10

Once You've Experienced Your Breakthrough, What Remains is the Dyamond in the Rough

DYAMOND IN THE ROUGH MEDICAL OFFICE

Taylor, Dyamond L
MRN: ▮▮▮▮▮▮▮▮
DOB: 11/3/1994, Sex: F

Visit Information
2018 1:30 PM

Patient presents with:
DISCHARGE NOTE

Precipitating factor to treatment: Patient reports that she wanted to talk about "the reasons why I use drugs and not only focus on my drug use". In addition, patient explored family of origin issues that contribute to her adult relationships today; and identified that she was an adult child of an alcoholic and also described years of complex trauma experiences that impact her world view perspective today. Patient processed feelings about multi generational transmission of trauma including: sexual assault, substance abuse and mental illness.

Discharge Note: Patient reports that she has benefited from treatment. "I want to be a good mom." Patient exhibits large social media following and involvement. States that she plans to write a book about her life.

Case is closed effective immediately.

Pandora's Box

I've always thought deeply about why and how I ended up the way I did. I searched deep within for the strength and courage to be able to trace the scars that the people before me didn't even try to investigate. I came across a certain pattern while trying to understand my parents. I couldn't help but see both of my mother's and father's mommy and daddy issues get passed down to little ol' me and stemming from those deep abandonment issues were dismissed psychiatric needs and problematic borderline behavior.

Intergenerational trauma is unresolved pain that is passed down from generations. Either the trauma hasn't been acknowledged or it's been minimized, helping to avoid the pain rather than having to address it. Yet to be able to break the cycles of trauma that is passed down, you have to understand where it came from. While 'til this day, my mother has successfully basked in denial to pretend that she is content in life and quote-unquote living in the present. I myself have had to battle her own mother-daughter demons that she has subconsciously projected onto me throughout half of my life. The other half of my life, I have had to watch my father self-medicate with alcohol, crack, and crystal meth because of a transference of emotional and psychological instability from his own mother and father that was passed down to him which caused him to have deeply rooted self-esteem issues and judging from his incapability to be a father his damn self, a lack of self-efficacy.

Because my parents were too young to ever address their childhood trauma, they proceeded to trauma bond and ended up creating me. Sadly mistaken that I would fill their voids, I too had to grow up struggling from unresolved psychiatric needs. I too suffered from not knowing my worth, so I as well coped by masking my pain with drugs and reckless sex.

Only difference is that I knew I had to break the cycle. I endured numerous anxiety attacks when I decided to go against my therapist's request to "not go opening pandora's box" because I didn't believe her when she told me I shouldn't do it by myself. I thought she was just blowing me off because our session was coming to an end. So, of course, I went right ahead and did it anyway, causing myself to relive all the trauma I never thought I'd have to. I curated every piece I've ever written and eliminated those I felt didn't genuinely speak from the pit of my soul. I requested all mental health records and faced everything I had ever allowed to break me down, sacrificing my sanity to deal with the pain that came with acknowledging the root of it all.

Every part of my journey was worth the struggle because I realized: I am a victim but I do not have a victim mentality. What was left of me was empathy and forgiveness towards my parents and their parents. Allowing me to break the cycle for my daughter and to even bring self-awareness to my daughter, sisters, and peers. When people read my story I don't want them to feel sorry for me but to rather feel me and know that they are not alone. I want people to see that there is always an opportunity for growth through acceptance and forgiveness. Through my many experiences, I am able to write about the cycles of abuse and abandonment and truly express that there is light at the end of these dark moments. If my hurt can transform into someone else's strength, I will be a martyr for self-love! I want to be the contradiction to the idea of "hurt people hurt people" and show that hurt people can help people. I believe everybody has a story of their own to tell.

Most Dyamonds Are Found Deep Within Us

If it's one thing that my Aunt Nikki taught me, it was to never give another person the power to determine how you feel about yourself. While it took years to understand what my aunt meant when she said that to me, it took me even longer to accept and acknowledge that escapism could not and would not bury those emotions. I had to learn on my own that certain people did not love me, and I had to learn the hard way. It took the strength and patience that came from learning how to love myself to truly find out that it wasn't anything personal. For a lot of people were never taught how to even love themselves; and one of the many laws of love simply state that you cannot love anybody if you do not love yourself.

So, I've learned that you shouldn't hate anybody for not being capable of loving you because self-love wasn't instilled in them. More importantly, I learned that you can help, but you cannot heal someone who is broken. You may attempt to guide them, but a broken person has to seek the help they need if they truly want to heal themselves.

From a childhood of extreme confusion and vast pain to my teenage years of built up anger and a consistent, intense battle with self-doubt and hatred, it felt like it took me my whole life to figure this out. Even though I was extremely loving, I was not capable of loving those around me without eventually bringing some sort of pain to them because of the pain I was in.

In fact, it took many lonely dark nights and countless mistakes that turned into some of the greatest heartaches of my life for me to really sit down and look myself in the mirror and demand of myself unconditional self-love. I had to forgive myself for all the years I blamed myself for why my parents couldn't love me properly. I had to forgive myself for all the resentment and hatred I let fester in my heart towards them that I ultimately shifted myself. I had to forgive myself for all the nights I laid in my bathtub and inflicted pain to myself in attempts to cover other people's tracks with my own scars.

163

To all the Dyamonds in the Rough,

I pray that you know what great purpose you have in this wild wild world. I pray that you were taught and encouraged to love the beautiful skin you're in and if you weren't I pray that you do everything you can to break the cycle to make sure that your babies and little ones who enter your space are laced with extreme self-love and everlasting confidence. I pray that if you ever question your worth, you look to your angels and ancestors to guide and connect you to your heaven on earth assignment.

Once you reach the minimum capacity requirement of loving yourself, I pray you learn how to selfishly love yourself until you have reached your maximum capacity if possible. With that, you'll know how to always protect your physical, mental, and spiritual being at all cost. I beg God, that you never feel so low in life that you feel the need to harm yourself, but rather get the fuck up and stand up for yourself. Stand on your own and make it make sense.

It's 2020, so I'm not here to tell you how to live your life. I do know if there's anything I could tell you from my very own experience it would be to focus on yourself first and always pay attention to your own evolution because you don't ever want to lose sight and get caught up in the world's hype becoming someone you're not. All because you became obsessed with comparing yourself to others.

The hype will have you so distracted, that you sit there and subconsciously ignore the many transitions you need to go through in order to reflect and connect with your higher self. By the time you try to wake up, you'll realize that you've lost yourself, then anxiety will open the door for self-doubt, and ultimately bring fear. And now because you got caught up in the hype, you are afraid of who you are destined to be and that's called depression. I wouldn't wish it on anybody because depression is like the devil constantly on your back, playing with your mind.

DYAMOND IN THE ROUGH

That's why I can't stress how focus you have to be on yourself and paying attention to your evolution as a Goddess, whatever you may believe that to be. My prophecy as an unconditional mother, strong sister, and genuine friend is to never have your pure souls out on the street searching for what you can only find truly within. If there is anything, I want little girls, teenage girls, young women, and grown women to take and understand from sharing my truths, is that there is not one person in this world ever worth thinking about taking your life or even giving your life to. May it be your mother or father who ain't shit, your brother, sister, aunt or uncle who ain't shit. Your grandfathers and his father who wasn't shit. But more importantly, these lost men and women who don't even love themselves, because their mothers and fathers never thought it had to be instilled because they were always too caught up in their own dysfunction.

I pray my legacy will forever get those who don't believe in themselves enough to see they are capable of overcoming their trauma, so they can break the cycle that they thought broke them.

DYAMOND IN THE ROUGH

Definition of Dyamond in the Rough:
~~One having exceptional qualities or potential but lacking refinement or polish.~~

Once you've experienced your breakthrough, what remains is the Dyamond in the Rough. Through your journey of forgiveness and healing, the Dyamond will shine allowing all of your light to transpire as you transcend. The hardships that you endure require committed evolution and self-actualization. We must identify the greatest version of ourselves and reach for it with unconditional love then go out our own way to be further educated, grounded, and supported by our community. We need the love of our queen sisters, queen mothers and peers, so we can allow all the beauty in us to flourish. To bring a Dyamond to the light in a raw world of pebbles and rocks requires breaking cycles of abuse, shedding unhealthy habits and eliminating all that no longer serves you a purpose. We all have many stories of struggle, which are created in our own Dyamond shining process. The scars, stains and stories you behold are the gems that truly make you extraordinary. The value of a Dyamond is determined by you, and only you, the Dyamond.

Remember: The final product of your pain and trauma is a profound jewel that reflects your strength and resilience.

ACKNOWLEDGMENT
Grandma My husband Austin Mom Dad Papa Andre
Melvin Danielle Chloe Joshua Santana
Jaylen Sasha Brandee Dae Morgan TJ
Sandi Auntie BJ Uncle Sonny Aunt Nikki and Uncle Joey
Essence Mia Auntie Micale
Uncle Marcus Uncle Magic Uncle George
Mrs. Tate and Mrs. Gavia
Ashley Alissa
Emiko Love Aubri
Kyra Ashley CoCo Leilani
Cyera Amanda Vincent
P. Hill McFresh Creates MAX
And as always JIMMY (cuhs he'll always be Jimmy)

When it comes to everybody listed on this page, the term I love you is a complete understatement. I wouldn't even know where to begin and while most find that I'm extremely talented with the use of my words, I still cannot come up with the perfect ones to express my gratefulness for all the years of encouragement you given me when I was lost. More importantly, I cannot express how much I appreciate you all for all the unconditional love you've showed me when I didn't even know how to love myself.

Made in the USA
San Bernardino,
CA